PRAISE FOR *SOCIAL MEDIA SUCCESS FOR EVERY BRAND*

"If you've been waiting for the ultimate guide to navigating social media, here it is! Claire Diaz-Ortiz, my coauthor on *One Minute Mentoring* and one of *Fast Company*'s "Top Ten Social Media Mavens," condenses decades of social media savvy into sensible portions for digital communicators who want to expand their brand. Claire's smart, cheeky commentary and road-tested know-how will have you laughing as you learn from the best in the business. Whether you are a brand manager, a marketing specialist, or an optimistic entrepreneur, *Social Media Success for Every Brand* will help you—and your brand—win."

— KEN BLANCHARD, coauthor of *The New One Minute Manager®* and *Leading at a Higher Level*

"The amazing thing about social media is that it changes every day. The challenging thing about social media is that it changes every day. Thankfully, Claire Diaz-Ortiz is willing to jump into the tension of those two truths and wrestle out a smart way forward for all of us. If you're an expert at social media, read this book. If you're an amateur at social media, read this book. You'll be glad you did."

— JON ACUFF, *New York Times* bestselling author of *Finish: Give Yourself the Gift of Done*

"Looking for success in today's social media age? In *Social Media Success for Every Brand*, Claire Diaz-Ortiz lays out the long-term strategy that will get you there!"

— MARSHALL GOLDSMITH, #1 *New York Times* bestselling author of *Triggers*, *Mojo*, and *What Got You Here Won't Get You There*; Thinkers50 #1 Executive Coach and #1 Leadership Thinker

"It's easy to write a tweet about what you had for breakfast. It's hard to use social media to grow your brand and your business strategically. *Social Media Success for Every Brand* is the marketing guide that every brand needs to succeed in a digital world."

— DORIE CLARK, author of *Entrepreneurial You* and *Stand Out*; executive education faculty, Duke University Fuqua School of Business

"Newsflash: Social media marketing works. Bu[...] book to learn your path to success."

— DAVE KERPEN[...]

Likeable So[...]

D1041053

"Claire Diaz-Ortiz provides a pragmatic, soup-to-nuts primer on implementing the supremely effective StoryBrand marketing strategy on social media via her SHARE model, meshing this dynamic duo for being seen and heard by consumers on the most visible and visited platforms in the world. *Social Media Success for Every Brand* is smart, witty, and well-paced. An idealistic book, but one that thoroughly delivers the practical goods for effective social media marketing and does so coherently and economically. Disrupt your branding and marketing with Diaz-Ortiz's strategy, a must-read that will provide big returns on the time invested."

—WHITNEY JOHNSON, award-winning author of *Build an A-Team* and *Disrupt Yourself*

"What works on social media today is not what worked ten years ago. (And do you even know what worked ten years ago?) *Social Media Success for Every Brand* is the book to help you understand how to make social media marketing work once and for all."

—CHRIS LOCURTO, author and entrepreneur

SOCIAL MEDIA SUCCESS FOR EVERY BRAND

S O CIAL MEDIA SUCCESS FOR EVERY BRAND

THE FIVE STORYBRAND PILLARS THAT TURN POSTS INTO PROFITS

CLAIRE DIAZ-ORTIZ

HarperCollins Leadership

AN IMPRINT OF HarperCollins

Published by HarperCollins Leadership, an imprint of HarperCollins Focus LLC.

The author is represented by Ambassador Literary Agency, Nashville, TN.

Any internet addresses, phone numbers, or company or product information printed in this book are offered as a resource and are not intended in any way to be or to imply an endorsement by HarperCollins Leadership, nor does HarperCollins Leadership vouch for the existence, content, or services of these sites, phone numbers, companies, or products beyond the life of this book.

ISBN 978-1-4002-14987-6 (Ebook)
ISBN 978-1-4002-1496-9 (TP)

Library of Congress Cataloging-in-Publication Data

Library of Congress Control Number: 2019945647

Printed in the United States of America

19 20 21 22 23 LSC 10 9 8 7 6 5 4 3 2 1

To great brands and the builders behind them.

CONTENTS

CONTENTS

FOREWORD

Like most of us, I have a love/hate relationship with social media. I signed off of Facebook about ten years ago and have never signed back in. My team runs a Facebook page for me, but I've never visited it.

I also moved my Twitter app to the last swipe on my iPhone screen, so it's not so easy to find. Why? Because Twitter makes me mad and brings out the worst in me. Sometimes when I'm scrolling through Twitter, I feel like an audience member on *The Jerry Springer Show*. It's all I can do not to throw a chair.

I like Instagram because it's mostly pictures of peoples' kids or peoples' dogs or peoples' kids playing with their dogs. That and inspirational quotes. My favorite inspirational quotes are the ones of people quoting themselves. Or the ones in which a word is misspelled.

I might be a cynic.

I'm an introvert but not by choice. Back before social media, you had to show up at places in order to network. And I hated showing up at places. I never knew what to say. I had a friend who said to make more eye contact, so I did. I'd just stare into people's eyes, without speaking. I'm lucky I never ended up with a restraining order against me.

Later, another friend gave me a few questions to ask that always got the ball rolling. What's the next big thing you're looking forward to? What's one thing about your current job that still surprises you? Questions like that.

Once I went in to social events with a little plan, things got easier. I started to succeed a little bit. Then I discovered I wasn't so introverted—I just lacked a plan.

Similarly, in this book, Claire gives us a plan.

Like I said, I love and hate social media. I hate the part that feels like you're in competition with billions of other people to become famous. But I love the part that allows you to be known, in a small way, to thousands. I like telling people that my wife and I just saw a movie we enjoyed, or I just finished reading a book and I really liked it. I don't think there's anything narcissistic about that. Right? Did I mention I finish books? Follow me on Instagram, and I'll prove it.

Claire Diaz-Ortiz has helped me increase the love I have for social media and decrease the hate. And in significant percentages.

I like social media more now than I did before, both as a person and for my brand.

Because I like it more now, I use it more. And that has translated into greater sales for my company. StoryBrand has surpassed $10 million in annual sales, and I attribute about 20 percent of that to our social media platforms. And I attribute the success of those platforms to what Claire teaches in this book.

This isn't a book to read as much as it is a book to study. If you have a marketing team, I'd get each member a copy.

Two things were missing from my perspective about social media: (1) a philosophy and (2) a workable plan.

Think about that for a second. Do you have a social media philosophy? Do you have a social media plan?

If not, you likely love/hate/mostly hate social media too. But what if you could love it more? And what if it could help you grow your platform?

These days, the networking party we all should attend is happening on social media platforms. And it's okay not to be there, but it's going to cost us if we aren't. Claire Diaz-Ortiz helps us show up prepared and because we are prepared, we are more likely to succeed, and because we succeed, we're more likely to like it.

If this book changes you, it changes you into somebody who enjoys showing up at the party. It won't make you famous, but it will make you more happy. And everybody likes somebody who is happy.

See you at the party.

To your success,
DONALD MILLER
Bestselling author of *Building a StoryBrand*

WHY MARK CUBAN WON'T MAKE YOUR BRAND GO VIRAL

Not that the story need be long, but it will
take a long while to make it short.
—HENRY DAVID THOREAU

A start-up once asked me to help them relaunch their struggling brand and effectively market their story on social media.

The company had a pretty good product but pretty terrible marketing. I knew social media marketing would be instrumental to their success, and theirs sucked. There was great room for improvement.

After I spent many weeks on an in-depth launch strategy outlining how they could effectively build a powerful, long-term brand on social media, we met to talk through my plan. It was clear they hadn't read much of it. The parts they had read, they suggested they might do "later on down the road."

In the meeting one of the team members spoke up. He was ready to make his big point. "I just really think that if we can get Mark Cuban to tweet about us, we'll get lots of followers and blow up."

Other team members nodded. I had heard hints of this from them before. My plan had, in fact, spent dedicated time specifically addressing why this was highly unlikely to work and why setting this as a goal was a bad idea.

Another team member piped up: "Yeah, Claire, can you help us 'go viral'?"

It was not the first time a brand had asked me that question.

My username on Twitter is @claire. I was an early employee at the company, and news outlets have called me "The Woman Who Got the Pope on Twitter." I am also the first and likely only person to have the questionable idea to live-tweet my own child's birth, an event that incidentally did "go viral."

The start-up in question earnestly and misguidedly believed that if they could just get Mark Cuban to tweet about them, they would be on the road to success. Furthermore, they apparently had hired me with the idea that this is what great social media marketing looked like.

Needless to say, they never got off the ground.

To understand why, and what they could have done differently, you need to learn what it means to effectively use social media to amplify your brand's clear story and build a long-lasting movement around your product, service, or idea.

That is what this book is all about.

WHAT EVERYONE GETS WRONG ABOUT SOCIAL MEDIA

Imagine that you have been invited to a few different cocktail parties. You can choose which one you go to, but to save face you have to show up to at least one. If you want to make a good impression, you have to do more than just show up. You have to stand out.

In brainstorming ways to do so, you come up with a few ideas:

You can physically make an impact in the room. You can wear a bright red dress, maybe, or one of those enormous British hats. You can be clear in the way you speak and the message you convey so that people will understand you. You can talk at a normal volume and not engage in creepy close-talking. You can be authentic, perhaps occasionally going off-script if that deepens your connections. You can do something unexpectedly kind. You can ask questions. You can avoid long monologues and excessive bragging, and you can spend a lot of time listening. And most importantly, if only a dozen people show up, you can avoid focusing your energy on wondering where everyone *else* is and trying to convince random passersby to come in and eat all the cheese.

Cocktail parties are like social media platforms.

At a cocktail party, the point is not to rush up to your old boss's co-worker's ex-husband, who is just trying to unwind with some onion dip after a long day, and annoyingly try to close a sale on your latest widget. The point is to meet people in a low-pressure environment, engage, and potentially exchange contact information to follow up on later if you're both up to it.

Similarly, successful social media strategy isn't about convincing Mark Cuban to retweet you, "going viral," or pushing your product down people's throats. Instead, the goal of social media for any brand should be to pique existing and potential followers' interest enough to get them to *further* engage by moving up something I call *the engagement ladder*.

Social media is a cocktail party full of folks, and your brand's success depends on being the one person at the party everyone wants to talk to.

I WENT VIRAL AND ALL I GOT WAS THIS LOUSY ONESIE

When I live-tweeted my daughter's birth, it went viral. Since I gave birth three weeks early, many of my friends and family were particularly stunned to hear about @Lucia entering the world from the anchors on *Good Morning America*.

A ton of major news sources in more than a dozen countries covered the story. At one point in the day, my daughter and I were the main story on Yahoo's *homepage*. Our picture appeared on all the morning shows. Conan O'Brien joked about us in his opening monologue.

To understand why this event went viral, you need to know exactly what happened.

I went into labor in the middle of

the night in my home in Argentina, but at the time I didn't know it was labor. As is my fashion, I turned to Google, and then I turned to Twitter to document my Googling.[1]

 @claire
Currently Googling: Did my water just break? #labor

My first tweet was a pattern-breaker on a slow Friday night of social media, and it also reeked of authenticity. It's hard to fake live-tweet your child's birth. People also noticed it because most don't tweet such questions.

At first, some friends and followers who happened to be awake in their time zone took note and started following along with my tweets. Some started retweeting. A journalist on Twitter saw it and sent it to some of his friends. Then the first news article appeared. Then the second. Within hours, as people began to wake up in time zones in the US, key celebrities began tweeting about it, and the momentum began to really pick up. Despite some pain-related breaks, I was having fun with it, and I snuck my iPhone into the operating room (it was not allowed in my Argentine hospital) to keep tweeting.

It was a developing story, and people wanted to know what was going to happen. It pulled at all the heartstrings. A first-time dad! A car broken down on the way to the hospital! A taxi driver who was not impressed! A new mother with great nails! As more and more news outlets around the world picked it up, more and more celebrities and more and more of their followers were talking about this strange developing story. Then it hit the morning shows, spreading via television, and then the late-night shows, keeping the story reverberating for days. It would take months for latecomers to get up to speed and stop tweeting me congratulations on my then six-month old. Years later, I still see retweets from time to time.

It was wildly fun, and alongside a bunch of random people on the internet, I had one heck of a good time at the party.

What happened after the live-tweeting of my daughter's birth went viral?

Nothing.

The day *after* I went viral was probably the day the internet went wild for that Christian girl who decided to never wear leggings again for religious reasons, or the man who stapled a cardboard box on his lawn mower to plow the snow in his yard.

And that is precisely what happens most of the time when things go viral.

Unless there is a careful *plan* for maximizing the attention from a focused burst of intense social media and a *purpose* for doing so, going viral won't do anything.

I did not have any motive for going viral with my daughter's birth. I did not have a company selling handcrafted wooden baby toys, nor had I written a parenting book on babies in the digital age. Neither did I maximize the attention by agreeing to appear on any of the morning shows that asked me to do so only hours after I became a ragged new mother. I had no mechanism for capturing the short-term attention and turning it into long-term followers. In short, there was no *engagement ladder* in place to capture any of the attention and lead anyone from A to Z.

All of this was more than okay with me. Live-tweeting the birth of my first child was something spontaneous I did for fun, regardless of the highly unexpected outcome. Plus, my mother got a kick out it.

Unfortunately, many brands don't realize the reality of going viral, so they spend lots of time and energy trying to do so. Similarly, some people spend lots of time and energy trying to train uncooperative pets.

Snakes are notoriously untrainable. Does that mean that people don't try?

Of course not. The crazy lady next door to you has one, and she's been "training" him for years! When you reluctantly bump into her in your bathrobe on Sunday, she always says, "Watch how Fluffy can help you get your newspaper."

While it's true that Fluffy has occasionally gone in the correct direction of the Sunday *New York Times*, it only happens once in every twenty Sundays. And when it does happen, that is no predictor of what will happen *next* week. Despite your neighbor's beliefs, there is no objective upward progression to Fluffy's abilities.

And that's exactly what going viral is like for brands. Even when lots of marketing dollars are involved, it's highly unpredictable. Have you ever heard of Olive Garden's Random Act of Pasta?[2] Or eBay's "Windorphins"? Microsoft Vista's Show Us Your Wow? The Cheetos Orange Underground? What about the Gusher eyeball that made mommy bloggers vomit?[3]

No, no, no, no, and no. And that's probably a good thing.

WHY GOING VIRAL IS NOT A STRATEGY

One of the biggest problems with that start-up that wanted Mark Cuban to make them "go viral" was not that they fantasized about going viral, but rather that they saw this as an *actual strategy*. And they are not alone. Billion-dollar organizations, small businesses, and individual celebrities have come to me over the years looking to improve their social media strategy. Many times, their current plan is a dressed-up version of trying to get Mark Cuban to tweet about them.

Brands know that social media matters but don't know how to powerfully use it. They end up running their marketing based on the flawed notion that going viral is both a strategy and a solution, like setting a goal to win a gold medal in the Olympics if you are a great figure skater: it's very *hard* to do but it's possible. If you are exceptional and have enough talent and work hard enough and hire the right coaches, you have a good shot of making it to Olympic Village, where you can get some free puffy jackets.

Unfortunately, going viral is nothing like this.

Instead, setting a goal to go viral is like setting a goal to win the annual holiday bingo game at your grandmother's retirement home. You can stack the odds in your favor to win big by being good at bingo and buying lots of cards to play on and by choosing the annual big-ticket game and not the small monthly ones, but at the end of the day it's not up to you. Because you just never know. Maybe there will be an unusually high number of players this year, or maybe the switch to brand-name hearing aid batteries means that more folks will hear the bingo caller, or maybe the luck of the number draw isn't on your side. Unfortunately, even if you *do* win, you have no idea if Grandma's retirement home is giving out the Mexican cruise or the new recliner as this year's prize. And, saddest of all, if Grandma's health declines, you can't come back next year. #wompwomp

When it comes to "going viral," there is no guarantee that it will get you closer to where you want to go, and there are way too many variables outside of your control to make this a worthwhile goal.

STOP TRYING TO GO VIRAL—START TRYING TO BUILD A BRAND

This doesn't mean you should hang up your hat and pull your brand off of social media. Social media is an incredibly effective way to share your message, and learning to do it well is key to your marketing success. Furthermore, the ubiquity of social media means that it is your brand's best opportunity to be as clear as possible *as often* as possible. Plus, it's free. (In this book we'll focus on organic social media, although we'll share some ideas about paid social media marketing as well.)

Instead of wasting your time and money on trying to go viral, you need to learn the surefire way to build a successful brand on social media. The hidden benefit of this strategy is that if you do go viral, you will be able to capitalize on it.

In this book we'll be exploring exactly how to do this.

Let me tell you the story of another client I once had who came to me to help her firm improve their marketing.

Diane (name changed to protect the innocent) ran a software company in the leadership and development space that sold online training platforms to human resources (HR) departments to help develop and motivate employees at large enterprises. The average purchase price for an annual license was more than $150,000 and the buyer was typically a senior-level executive.

Diane was extremely reluctant to spend any time on social media, so I asked her to explain how she usually gets sales. She said it was through networking and connections. Someone she knows leads to someone she knows leads to someone who buys. There are a lot of lunches.

She told me the story of how she got a recent client. Thanks to the reputation she has built up in the space, a local event asked her to come speak. Although they didn't pay her, she agreed because she knew it could be a good networking opportunity. An HR person in the audience enjoyed her talk, came up to her afterward, and asked her to lunch. He then hired Diane to speak to the employees of his pharmaceutical company. After another lunch with someone more senior, the company purchased a license. Diane hopes they will renew for many years to come.

Now, just imagine for a moment that Diane had been using the brand marketing power of social media throughout this process. Maybe she would've realized she was already connected with the HR person on LinkedIn through someone else, thus reinforcing their connection at lunch ("You *also* worked with crazy Carol?") or even cutting out the need for one of the later steps in the journey to close the sale. Maybe there were more people in the audience that day who didn't have time for lunch but could have connected with her online afterward, potentially leading to more opportunities. Or maybe by regularly sharing free content on social media Diane would get many more invitations to talk at free events just like this one, which could replicate this entire process.

As she told me the story, she kept coming back to the same questions: Should she really bother with social media marketing? Does it lead to sales? Shouldn't she just focus on trying to sell to the senior-level executive who buys the big-ticket item?

This is the story I should have told her. Or rather, this is how Wes does it.

SIX FIGURES FROM A SINGLE TWEET

These days, Wes Gay is a successful StoryBrand Guide who runs a StoryBrand Certified Agency (see appendix 3 for more information) called Wayfinder Consulting.[4]

In 2016, things were different. Back then, Wes was unemployed and living with his wife, two-year-old, newborn, and seventy-five-pound dog in the cramped second floor of his mother-in-law's house. Almost everything he owned was in storage.

Wes had unsuccessfully applied to more than fifty jobs in marketing. One time, he finally reached the second-round interview for a job he really wanted. It paid only $24,000 a year and probably wouldn't have been enough money to get his family out of his mother-in-law's. In the end, it was a moot point because the company never called him back.

All the while, he kept working on building his personal brand online as a marketing expert with an eye for helping businesses reach millennials. He knew that most companies didn't know how to effectively engage the largest generation in the workforce with their marketing. He did. No matter where his career went next, he knew that establishing his expertise online was important, so he continued to create quality content and share it via social media.

One day he wrote a blog post about millennials, which caught the attention of a *Forbes* editor looking for contributors for a new channel focused on millennials. She asked Wes to write a piece for *Forbes*, and he jumped at the chance. After a few unpaid posts on *Forbes*, he was offered the chance to become a regular contributor and provide a handful of pieces a month at a couple hundred dollars per piece. It wasn't much, but he agreed.

"When you are unemployed and living at your mother-in-law's, you'll do anything," he wisely said.

Around this time, he saw a tweet from Pushpay, a large technology company that offers mobile engagement solutions for churches and nonprofits. The tweet offered a free downloadable guide to pastors and church leaders to help them engage with millennials.[5]

 **@pushpay**
Pastors & Church Leaders The Ultimate Guide to Engaging
Millennials: Click Here for Your Free eBook!

Wes immediately had an idea of how he could help. In addition to his expertise with millennials, he was a former pastor and had worked on marketing with a number of churches. He wrote back.[6]

 @wesgay
I'm a @Forbes contributor w/a focus on Millennials. Also a
pastor. I think we could work together on this topic

The director of digital at Pushpay soon reached out:[7]

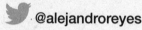 **@alejandroreyes**
Hi Wes. Thank you for reaching out to us. I'm the Director of
Digital & would love to chat . . .

Wes and Alejandro, the director of digital at Pushpay, set up a video call. Shortly thereafter, Alejandro invited Wes to speak on a panel at an upcoming event with John Maxwell and Bob Goff. Chris Heaslip, the CEO of Pushpay, was in the room alongside Pushpay's director of content marketing and the director of events. They all liked what Wes had to say. Later, they asked Wes to write and speak at another event, which then led to a larger contract.

Then Wes sent another tweet. This time he asked his followers if they thought he should get an MBA to further his marketing career. Chris Heaslip, Pushpay's CEO, responded. He suggested that Wes come to Seattle to meet with him. Wes soon went from on-and-off projects to a regular consulting gig working on several key projects to help scale the company.

In his first year working for Pushpay, Wes made over six figures. How did he do it?

Through the power of brand marketing.

THE THREE KEYS TO UNDERSTANDING SOCIAL MEDIA MARKETING: BRAND MARKETING, DIRECT MARKETING, AND THE ENGAGEMENT LADDER

BRAND MARKETING AND DIRECT MARKETING

If your brand wants to succeed on social media, it is essential that you first understand that there are two different kinds of marketing: *brand marketing* and *direct marketing*.

Brand marketing includes things like digital media, social media, and PR, and its primary goals are awareness and engagement. Building reputation and community are other goals.[8]

In contrast, the entire goal of direct marketing (also known as direct-response marketing) is to make a sale.

Brand marketing lays the groundwork for direct marketing, and you need brand marketing in order to execute effective direct marketing.

Jason Falls, the founder of Social Media Explorer, explains how brand marketing perfectly prepares the customer for the direct-marketing call to action when it comes time to close a sale. "If the prospective audience is aware, thinks positively of and has a previous interaction or relationship with a company, it is infinitely more likely to CHOOSE to BUY from that company when it finds itself in the buying mode. When presented with the direct marketing communication, it will say 'Yes' with more frequency."[9]

Let's go back to Diane, my client who sold the $150,000 software licenses, wasn't using social media marketing, and doubted social media could be of use. By the time Diane gave the speech that led to the meeting that led to *another* speech that led to *another* meeting, she had already prepared the client through multiple exposures to her work to *choose to buy*. She instinctively knew that she needed brand marketing to help her get to the point where she could close a deal with a senior level executive. After all, there is no amount she can pay Facebook to run a one-time ad that would convince a senior level executive at the pharmaceutical company to hand over a check for $150,000!

Amazingly, as I told Diane, she was *already doing brand marketing* without realizing it. She just needed to work on doing it more strategically and consistently on social media. In her case, when she said she had been invited to deliver that first speech because of the "reputation" she had built up, she was referring to more than fifteen years of blog posts, podcast interviews, and even some (limited) social media. She had accidentally been doing brand marketing all along. Furthermore, that was the entire reason she got invited to give that speech in the first place!

Quite simply, Diane needed the brand awareness she had built through brand marketing to lay the groundwork for her *direct* marketing call to action. And she would need it again. This time, though, I told her we would create a strategic, intentional social media marketing plan that would be wildly more effective than her "accidental" plan.

Let's look at an example of what happens when you don't do this.

Allison Fallon is a bestselling author and writing coach. As part of her work, she runs live workshops. Last year she paid a bunch of money to a firm to do some marketing work for her. They did a terrible job. Guess why? They ignored brand marketing and went straight to direct marketing. In this case, they ran cold social media ads to people who had never heard of Allison, inviting them to pay a bunch of money to fly across the country to come to a live event with her. The ads did terribly because they completely ignored that important thing I mentioned earlier: *the engagement ladder.* The engagement ladder is what takes people from brand marketing to direct marketing. A couple people did buy tickets to her event, but with no brand marketing the results were so inconsistent and expensive that they could never produce a profitable workshop.

In the example of Wes Gay, by concentrating on his own brand marketing he was able to lead his potential "customers" (first *Forbes*, then Pushpay) up the engagement ladder to hire him. In the situation of my client selling $150,000 licenses, she realized she was closing her sales because of brand marketing, which helped clients choose her when it came time for direct marketing. In Allison's case, by ignoring brand marketing and the engagement ladder, the direct marketing failed.

THE ENGAGEMENT LADDER

Let's look at exactly what the engagement ladder is and why it matters.

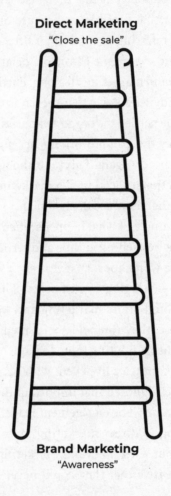

Direct Marketing
"Close the sale"

Brand Marketing
"Awareness"

Remember the cocktail party? You don't negotiate business deals at a cocktail party. Instead, you make every effort to be charming and memorable to create a connection to get the meeting that will eventually lead to a negotiation. Just like a cocktail party, the goal in social media is to stand out (aka "brand marketing"), so you can lead a potential customer up the engagement ladder to ultimately close a sale (aka "direct marketing").

Engagement ladders can vary, but here is an example of what a brand's ideal engagement ladder might look like:

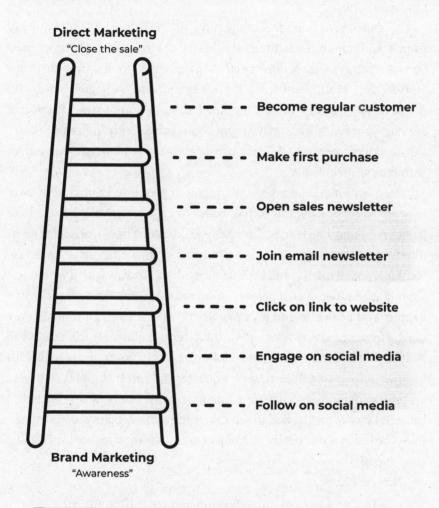

Direct Marketing
"Close the sale"

- - - - Become regular customer

- - - - Make first purchase

- - - - Open sales newsletter

- - - - Join email newsletter

- - - - Click on link to website

- - - - Engage on social media

- - - - Follow on social media

Brand Marketing
"Awareness"

> If you learn better by video, access a free five-video minicourse at SocialMediaMadeSimple.com.

Remember that once your customer is on the ladder and progressing up to higher rungs, the earlier rungs still matter. Otherwise, the whole ladder will fall down. If you get to the third rung on a ladder, that doesn't mean I can cut out the first rung and you'd still be standing. Similarly, if a customer makes a first purchase but unsubscribes from all email updates and unfollows you on social media, it will be very hard to sell to him again online.

Is it possible to skip some of the rungs on the ladder and jump quickly from brand marketing to direct marketing to close the sale? Sometimes. Some customers simply don't need as many touch points. (Impulse buys are a perfect example of this.) If your brand randomly goes viral, you might be able to skip some rungs for a brief period of time. If you are famous, your brand awareness might be so permanently high that you are able to skip some rungs. (That's why brands try to associate themselves with famous people.)

But even when brands go viral or famous people sell things, the closer they are to replicating the actual ladder of engagement the better. Take Jessica Alba and The Honest Company. Jessica Alba has an on-point ubiquitous brand message about being a mom dedicated to healthy living. Her blog, social media, and PR efforts work in tandem with The Honest Company's ladder of engagement to consistently empower people to live happily and healthily and give people the safe, effective products they need. Her company is worth almost a billion dollars.[10] In contrast, Rob Kardashian is brother to the most followed Instastars on the planet, with his own respectable following of a quarter million Instagram followers and sisters dedicated to tweeting him to success. But he was in such dire financial straits that he had to sell his failing sock company to his mom.[11] Rob Kardashian was probably not a great spokesman for socks. Does he wear them?

No one knows.

THE SHARE MODEL FOR SOCIAL MEDIA MARKETING SUCCESS

CHAPTER 1

THE SHARE MODEL: AN OVERVIEW

We've talked about what you need to know to be successful at social media marketing. Now let's look at exactly how to do it using the SHARE model. SHARE stands for *story, how, audience, reach*, and *excellence*. Here is a quick overview of how every brand can use the SHARE model to succeed. In the chapters that follow, we will dive deep into each step.

STORY

Use your StoryBrand BrandScript on social media to open the story gap, move your followers up an engagement ladder, and close the story gap when you call them to take action.

Remember:

- The first step in the SHARE model is *story*. Content is queen, and the content for your social media marketing comes from your StoryBrand BrandScript.
- Social media marketing is usually *brand marketing*, not *direct marketing*. That means that most of the time your goal is not an immediate sale.
- Effective social media marketing should always *open the story gap*,

move followers up an *engagement ladder*, and then *close the story gap* with a *call to action*.

- Your *social media bank account* only thrives with give-and-take. Remember the 80/20 rule. Deposit value 80 percent of the time by opening the story gap with your content. Then, 20 percent of the time make a withdrawal by closing the story gap with a call to action.
- To balance your *social media budget*, vary the types of content you deposit and withdraw. Content should come from different content envelopes, including things like curated content, original content, articles, quotations, statistics, testimonials, direct calls to action, transitional calls to action, impactful images, selfies, video, etc.

HOW

Learn the practical logistics of *how* to post your content.

Remember:

- Take the *Social Media Brand Evaluation* to determine your brand's priority social media platforms (see appendix 2). Concentrate on the platforms that matter most to your brand.
- To decide how many accounts you need on each platform, remember that the fewer accounts you have, the better.
- *Who* posts matters less than you think. *When* to post matters more. Time of day, day of the week, and season of the year are all considerations.
- Third-party tools can help with scheduling, curating, and analytics. Hootsuite, Buffer, Sprout Social, and Sendible are all good platforms that offer different benefits.
- Consistency is important. Ensure that you create a *social media schedule* and *social media editorial calendar* that work for your audience and your brand's bandwidth.
- Use pattern disruption and selective break-taking to your advantage.

AUDIENCE

Your social media marketing should be about your *audience*, not your brand.

Remember:

- Your brand is not your hero; your customer is.
- Your customer (or potential customer) is your follower. Reframe your social media account to make it about them.
- Cultivate empathy on social media matters to build a relationship with your customers and reach long-term success. Remember this equation: Empathy + Connection = Social Media Engagement.
- Generate empathy (and engagement) by telling a great story, helping someone, and asking questions.
- Don't post and ghost. Great social media marketing requires real-time connection and engagement with your audience.

REACH

To amplify your brand on social media, it's important to expand your *reach*.

Remember:

- Craft a killer social media profile that increases your authority and opens the story gap by using your BrandScript.
- Prioritize your existing social media tribe over new followers every day of the week.
- The three ways to get new followers on social media are to create great content, use influencer marketing, or pay for advertising to boost either of those strategies.
- Great hashtags can put great content on steroids. When crafting

a hashtag, be as general as you can without using a term people already associate with something else.

- Concentrate on reaching influencers in a way they like. Remember that it's a long-tail game that relies on finding the right niche, finding the right influencer, and engaging with them over time.

EXCELLENCE

Fine-tune your social media marketing efforts to reach long-term *excellence*.

Remember:

- Always ask yourself how you can get followers to want in on your story.
- The real-time nature of social media means that you don't always know what's going to happen. Make that a good thing.
- On social media, it's about rolling with the punches. If your brand makes a social media mistake, own up to it. Fast.
- Social media gives your customers a public place to share their grievances. Sometimes they will do just that. If the comments aren't offensive, let the dialogue take place, and don't delete the negative content. Whenever you can, try to turn a negative conversation into a positive one.

If you learn better by video, access a free five-video minicourse at SocialMediaMadeSimple.com.

CHAPTER 2

STORY: TELLING A GREAT SOCIAL MEDIA STORY

The SHARE model for social media marketing success builds off the StoryBrand 7-Part Framework (SB7), a marketing approach that thousands of companies of all sizes have used to clarify their message.

That's why the first step in the SHARE model is *story*. Your brand needs a great social media story, and that comes from your StoryBrand BrandScript.

If you're new to StoryBrand, let's take a refresher course on The StoryBrand 7-Part Framework (SB7) to get you the BrandScript you need to move forward.

THE SIMPLE SB7 FRAMEWORK

People don't buy the best products; they buy the products they can understand the fastest.
—DONALD MILLER, *BUILDING A STORYBRAND*

Your brand's biggest enemy is noise. As such, your brand's greatest opportunity is to use clear marketing to cut through the noise to reach your customer. These days, reaching your customer doesn't mean you have to wait for them to walk by your store or receive your monthly direct mailer. The ubiquity of social media and the amount of time your potential customers spend on it mean that your brand has countless opportunities *every day* to show your customer that you are just what she needs to solve her problem.

You do that with a clear story.

The StoryBrand 7-Part Framework, or SB7, is a communication and marketing formula created by Donald Miller, CEO of StoryBrand. Thousands of companies have used this formula to boost their marketing. It works because it appeals to our most basic understanding of story as a means to captivate an audience. In fact, some version of this formula has been used for thousands of years to tell stories. When you understand how it works, you can then create your own brand's story (or StoryBrand BrandScript) to engage your customers and grow your business.

In this chapter, I'll give an overview of the framework. You can dive much further into this process in Donald Miller's bestselling book *Building a StoryBrand: Clarify Your Message So Customers Will Listen.*

According to the SB7 Framework, pretty much every good story you've ever heard breaks down into the following seven plot points:

A *character* who wants something encounters a *problem* before they can get it. At the peak of their despair, a *guide* steps into their lives, gives them a *plan*, and *calls them to action*. That action helps them avoid *failure* and ends in *success*.[1]

As you think about the good stories you know, you'll see that some flexibility exists, but for the most part, these seven plot points are always there when it comes to a successful story. (Stories that don't follow this formula, like indie movies, may be critically approved but will fail at the box office.)

Let's see how it works in a story we all know well. Then we can put it into a marketing context.

Enter a woman known to children and former children everywhere.

Cinderella, our *character*, leads a miserable life in a cold attic, sweeping cinders while her stepsisters sit downstairs in the warmth making fun of her. One day a duke invites them all to a ball. Cinderella has a *problem*: she wants to go but has nothing to wear! Amazingly, a fairy godmother *guide* flies in with a *plan*. With the flick of her wand, she turns Cinderella's rags into a beautiful dress and the rat into a driver and the pumpkin into a carriage, and *calls Cinderella to action*. "Go! Enjoy! But remember, all of this is only on loan until midnight!" Enter drama when Cinderella loses track of the time and is thisclose to not executing on the plan and *failing* (she loses her shoe as she is racing out of the castle at midnight). Ultimately, after a hefty dose of suspense, Cinderella gets the true love and happiness she seeks. *Success!*

Here it is written out on a StoryBrand grid:

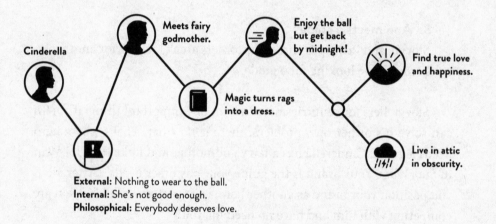

External: Nothing to wear to the ball.
Internal: She's not good enough.
Philosophical: Everybody deserves love.

We'll now explore the seven elements of the SB7 Framework more closely to understand how they relate to marketing and why your brand should create a story about itself that is just as good as the Cinderella story.

1. The character

StoryBrand Principal One: The customer is the hero, not your brand.

Let's get the startling stuff out of the way first. Your brand is not the hero. Your customer is. Figuring out who the hero is and what she wants is essential.

2. Has a problem

StoryBrand Principle Two: Companies tend to sell solutions to external problems, but customers buy solutions to internal problems.

A customer is motivated to buy something to solve a problem. If your brand can solve his problem, you'll win his business. In story and in marketing there are three levels of problems: external, internal, and philosophical. The deeper the problem you try to solve for your customer, the more you will endear yourself.

3. And meets a guide

StoryBrand Principle Three: Customers aren't looking for another hero; they're looking for a guide.

Storytellers for centuries have known one important thing: if a hero can solve his or her own problem, there is no story. That's why a hero needs a guide. Cinderella has a fairy godmother and Luke has Obi-Wan in *Star Wars*. Your brand is the guide your customer needs. (After all, if you position your brand as another hero, your customer will feel you are competing with him and have no need for you.)

4. Who gives them a plan

StoryBrand Principle Four: Customers trust a guide who has a plan.

Even if you know who your customer is and what she wants, she won't buy from you unless you have a plan in place that she can follow to take action. If the fairy godmother had shown up but didn't have a plan for what to do next, there's no way Cinderella would have agreed to ride off in a former vegetable.

5. And calls them to action

StoryBrand Principle Five: Customers do not take action unless they are challenged to take action.

Just like humans in real life, characters in stories don't take action unless they are challenged to. Your brand needs to develop a call to action in your messaging to ensure that you are motivating your potential customer to take the next step.

6. That helps them avoid failure

StoryBrand Principle Six: Every human being is trying to avoid a tragic ending.

"What's at stake?" is the critical question in every fairy tale and brand story. The goal is to paint enough of a portrait of what failure looks like to ensure your customer takes action. But don't go too low.

7. And ends in success.

StoryBrand Principle Seven: Never assume people understand how your brand can change their lives. Tell them.

Don't leave "happily ever after" to the imagination. Your brand must be clear about how you can really help people. As Donald Miller says, "Everybody wants to be taken somewhere. If we don't tell people where we are taking them they will engage another brand."[2]

Here is another example of the SB7 Framework in a popular story. This time it's *Star Wars:*[3]

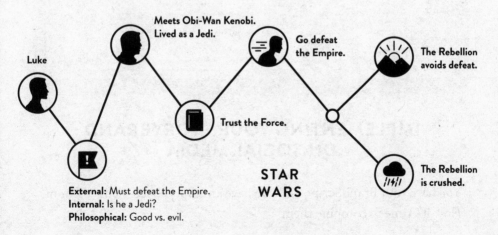

Luke

Meets Obi-Wan Kenobi.
Lived as a Jedi.

Go defeat
the Empire.

The Rebellion
avoids defeat.

Trust the Force.

External: Must defeat the Empire.
Internal: Is he a Jedi?
Philosophical: Good vs. evil.

STAR WARS

The Rebellion
is crushed.

So that's the overview of the SB7 Framework. Remember that at first glance it may seem that some great marketing campaigns don't use this. Look closer. They probably are doing it so well that you can't tell.

As previously mentioned, if you want to delve deeper into how to create your BrandScript, read Donald Miller's bestselling book *Building a StoryBrand*.

Now it's your turn to use SB7 with your own business. See appendix 3 for information on how to download your free StoryBrand BrandScript tool to help simplify the process.[4] Once you have a BrandScript you are pleased with, then it's time to move on to the rest of the book.

IMPLEMENTING YOUR STORYBRAND ON SOCIAL MEDIA

You have your BrandScript, and you have an empty social media account. Now it's time to combine them!

(Insert record scratch.)

Until now, brands who have gone through the StoryBrand process have often struggled to understand how to implement their BrandScript on social media. This book solves that problem.

Let's start by remembering that your BrandScript is your overarching guide for everything related to your brand's marketing. How you apply it on social media is up to the SHARE model.

THE SOCIAL MEDIA BANK ACCOUNT

In the beginning of this book, we talked about what it's like when the worst guy at the cocktail party corners you next to the onion dip. The guy who only talks about himself and then tries to get you to buy his latest widget, listen to his band's new song, or deeply inhale his favorite healing essential oil. It sucks to get stuck in a conversation with that guy.

After reading the introduction, you now understand the biggest mistake brands make on social media is to use it only for direct marketing, and you can see why it's a bad idea to use your social media accounts to only blast out the content and calls to action in your BrandScript all day.

In other words, don't be that guy.

Instead, think of each of your social media accounts like a bank account. To stay in the black and grow over time, you need to consistently deposit more in the account than you withdraw. Making a deposit into your social media bank account is what you do when you give followers valuable content that gets them on, keeps them on, or organically moves them up your engagement ladder. In StoryBrand terms, this is also called *opening the story gap.*

Withdrawing from your social media bank account is what you do when you ask a follower to take action or *close the story gap.* This may be a direct call to action like, "Buy Neon Slime Today!" Or it may be a transitional call to action and a way to intentionally move them up the engagement ladder to get closer to closing the story gap later on. For example, "Download My Quick Guide to Making Neon Slime" would be one good way to direct your followers to go up your engagement ladder to one day become an ideal neon slime customer.

Remember the cardinal rule is that you always need to be depositing more than you withdraw.

My rule of thumb is to follow the 80/20 rule, or the Pareto principle, "a theory maintaining that 80 percent of the output from a given situation or system is determined by 20 percent of the input."[5]

If we apply this to social media, we see that we can "sell" our followers 20 percent of the time to reap the majority of the sales results. In other words, 80 percent of the time within the course of the month you want to be making deposits by curating or creating valuable content to open the story gap. Then, 20 percent of the time you want to be making withdrawals in the form of a direct call to action or transitional call to action to close the story gap.

(In the next chapter we'll look at exactly how this will look on a social media calendar.) For now, remember that sometimes unexpected things happen. Let's say your manufacturer made a mistake and instead of neon slime you now have one thousand extra jars of brown slime on your hands that you need to get rid of. You have to be prepared to go in the hole for emergencies. You can schedule extra withdrawals from your social media accounts in the form of calls to action to sell off the discounted slime.

To keep your social media accounts in the black, though, you'll need to do some extra work to get new deposits. In short, if you need to make extra withdrawals one month from your social media account, then simply work hard to make extra deposits as well.

THE SOCIAL MEDIA BUDGET

Now that you've got a bank account for each of your social media platforms, you'll need a social media budget to match. On social media, you need a budget for your deposits as well as for your withdrawals.

Since a typical financial budget is broken down into specific budget categories (food, housing, clothes, etc.), we'll do the same thing for our social media budgets. Here are examples of the many types of content categories that exist on social media. Some of these will overlap, as you will see:

- original content you create
- curated content from other sources
- direct calls to action
- transitional calls to action
- articles, blog posts, podcast episodes
- quotations
- statistics
- testimonials
- impactful images
- case studies
- selfies that don't suck
- recorded videos
- live videos

Importantly, your social media accounts require different types of content deposits and withdrawals to keep them thriving and growing over time.

If you post all curated statistics for one month, for example, your account will be over-indexed in that area and your followers may start getting bored. Despite your beauty, you may not be able to post selfies every day without followers getting sick of your face and unfollowing you. This is no different than putting together a personal budget. If you set aside money only for new clothes, you will soon be homeless and hungry. In other words, you will fail. But if you create a unique combination of budget categories that fits your unique needs and follow that budget, you will be successful.

That's why you need to first identify the key content categories or *content envelopes* for your brand.[6] Think about what types of content work best for your followers. If you are a local newspaper, you will want more curated article content than selfies. If you are a fitness instructor, your followers will likely want way more selfies than statistics. If you are a nonprofit bringing clean water to India, powerful statistics *and* impactful images might both be equally important. Go straight back to your BrandScript. Who is your character, after all? If you are Tesla, you appeal to high-end tech aficionadas who may want more flashy videos of your latest innovation in top-opening wing doors. If you are Volvo, car-pooling dads who care about car safety might like some calming Swedish statistics.

Don't worry if you're not exactly sure what will work. You will be refining this process over time.

In the next chapter we'll explore how to budget each type of content to share according to the social media schedule you develop and your social media editorial calendar. That means that each month, for example, you will put all your planned content into different content envelopes. Over the course of the month you follow your social media editorial calendar to make your deposits and withdrawals until every content envelope is empty.

EXACTLY WHAT TO POST ON SOCIAL MEDIA

Remember that your social media bank accounts require different types of content to keep them thriving. In your social media budget, you will want to allocate deposits to deliver value to your followers and offset the withdrawals you make when you close the story gap and call a follower to take action to bring them up the engagement ladder.

First let's look at exactly what type of content you can use for your deposits.

Content Withdrawals (20% of the time)		Content Deposits (80% of the time)	
I	**Content You Create**	**II**	**Content You Create**
	• Impactful Images • Selfies • Videos • Statistics • Articles, Blog Posts, and Podcast Episodes with calls to action		• Articles, Blog Posts, and Podcast Episodes • Quotations • Statistics • Impactful Images • Selfies That Don't Suck • Videos
III	**Curated Content**	**IV**	**Curated Content**
	• Testimonials • Quotations • Statistics • Impactful Images • Videos		• Articles, Blog Posts, and Podcast Episodes • Quotations • Statistics • Impactful Images • Videos

Content You Create (left vertical label, rows I and II)
Curated Content (left vertical label, rows III and IV)

20% of the Time   **80% of the Time**

CONTENT DEPOSITS: WHAT TO POST 80 PERCENT OF THE TIME

CURATED CONTENT (CONTENT DEPOSITS)

	Content Withdrawals (20% of the time)		Content Deposits (80% of the time)
Content You Create	**I** Content You Create • Impactful Images • Selfies • Videos • Statistics • Articles, Blog Posts, and Podcast Episodes with calls to action	**II** Content You Create • Articles, Blog Posts, and Podcast Episodes • Quotations • Statistics • Impactful Images • Selfies That Don't Suck • Videos	
Curated Content	**III** Curated Content • Testimonials • Quotations • Statistics • Impactful Images • Videos	**IV** Curated Content • Articles, Blog Posts, and Podcast Episodes • Quotations • Statistics • Impactful Images • Videos	
	20% of the Time		80% of the Time

To ensure that you aren't the guy at the cocktail party who everybody hates, it is important to listen to other people and let them talk. On social media, one of the key ways you do this is through curation.

Curating is all about highlighting other people, and it involves finding quality content from other sources and posting it to your followers. Primarily, you should do this by posting directly from your account, while referencing the original source or directing to the original source in the form of a link. Secondarily, you can do this when you repost, reshare, or retweet.[7]

Curated content should relate to your overall BrandScript. Are you a leadership expert with a BrandScript focused on helping busy executives balance their work and personal lives? Quality curated content on productivity is a great bet. Are you a gym with a BrandScript all about helping people get in shape? Content about health and fitness is your beat.

Here are some of the types of content you can curate:

- *Articles, blog posts, and podcast episodes*: These are the most common content to curate.
- *Quotations*: Quotations are hugely popular on social media, with or without accompanying images. Remember to cite.
- *Statistics*: Depending on your brand, statistics can be a great way to give value that others want to pass along.
- *Impactful images*: Powerful images do well on social media.
- *Videos*: Videos are one of the most highly engaged forms of social media posts.

Remember that not all types of content will work for all brands. A teddy bear company may not find statistics useful, and Tesla may not want to use inspirational quotes.

Now that you know the types of content that you can curate, here are some best practices for curating well:

Read content in your niche. To be a great curator, nothing beats being informed. The best way to find great items for curation is to read the online magazines, blogs, and news sources in your niche to stay up to date on what is going on and what people are talking about. Google Alerts can also be a great tool to direct you to articles or sites you aren't already familiar with. Offline material like books and magazines also work; it will just require more effort on your part to make the content fit for online posting.

Use a tool to help you curate. In the next chapter on *how*, we'll look at specific social media management tools that can make curation even easier. A tool like Buffer or Hootsuite can help you streamline the curation process by suggesting articles in your specific niche when you provide the tool with relevant keywords.

Be present on social media. A key way to make sure you're curating well is to spend time on the platform in question reading the posts of your followers to understand what they are talking about and resonating with. For example, each week on my own Twitter account I schedule a number of curated articles I find on blogs or that my social media posting tool suggests using the keywords I have provided, but I also find many more in my daily routine of reading my Twitter stream. Some I'll retweet directly, and others I'll save to post later.

Add your own take. Curating isn't just repeating the words of someone else. It's also about adding your own take when relevant. What was your big takeaway from the article you are sharing? How does this statistic make you think differently? Doing this some of the time is a good idea.

Change headlines when relevant. When curating you need to decide how you want to position the item in your own social media feed. This means either deciding to reuse the existing headline or to reposition it slightly with new wording in your own social media post. First, consider if you have added your own take or not. Then, think about your audience and what will most drive a click.

Reference the original source using the correct social media handle. It's critical to remember that you should reference the original content source using their social media handle if you want them to see it, engage with it, or expand the reach of the content. This is more important if the content comes from an individual or a smaller brand that is more likely to do so.

CONTENT YOU CREATE TO DEPOSIT

	Content Withdrawals *(20% of the time)*		Content Deposits *(80% of the time)*
I	**Content You Create**	**II**	**Content You Create**
Content You Create	• Impactful Images • Selfies • Videos • Statistics • Articles, Blog Posts, and Podcast Episodes with calls to action		• Articles, Blog Posts, and Podcast Episodes • Quotations • Statistics • Impactful Images • Selfies That Don't Suck • Videos
III	**Curated Content**	**IV**	**Curated Content**
Curated Content	• Testimonials • Quotations • Statistics • Impactful Images • Videos		• Articles, Blog Posts, and Podcast Episodes • Quotations • Statistics • Impactful Images • Videos
	20% of the Time		80% of the Time

Remember how we talked about not overdoing one type of content when it comes to your social media bank account?

When it comes to curation, it's critical to offer your own value as well. Back when Twitter was a small company and we were still shocked by some of the ways different people from all around the world were starting to use it, I got into the habit of emailing the whole company with interesting articles from around the world on a regular basis. I had signed up for daily Google Alerts about Twitter in dozens of countries, so I had some good material!

I genuinely loved the act of curating and wanted to share with my colleagues. Over time, the company grew and the global use cases exploded. So did my emails. One day, my boss warned that I should consider curating less and talking about my *own* contributions more. It was an important lesson in how curation can be perceived, and why original creation matters.

Here are some types of content you can *create* to deposit value. Remember to think back to the character in your BrandScript. What do they resonate with?

- *Articles, blog posts, and podcast episodes*: These are a critical way to deposit content.
- *Quotations*: Quotes and motivational phrases do well on social media. If relevant to your brand, write short, sharable content with or without accompanying media.
- *Statistics*: If your brand's followers value statistics and you have them, go for it.
- *Impactful images*: Powerful images of your own can deliver great value.
- *Selfies that don't suck*: For some brands and many celebrities, selfies are a regular way to open the story gap and deposit content that the follower wants, without calling a follower to take any kind of action. In other words, the selfie is the story.
- *Videos*: Videos are a classic way to tell a story to your social media following and open the story gap. Many of the live videos we see around us these days are based on this premise.

When it comes to depositing value, remember that it's also okay to go off-BrandScript at times. As we'll talk about more, oftentimes posting something unexpected is a great way to create a pattern break and connect with your followers. Did your city suffer a major storm and you want to send your well wishes to local customers? Did you find a funny video online that has nothing to do with anything, but you think your followers might love it (and engage with you as a result)? Doing this absolutely makes sense from time to time.

CONTENT WITHDRAWALS: WHAT TO POST 20 PERCENT OF THE TIME

Now that you understand how to make a content deposit, let's look at how to make a content withdrawal. On social media you make a withdrawal by posting the direct or the transitional call to action you created in your StoryBrand BrandScript. The goal is to close the story gap by moving someone up your engagement ladder.

Here's how to do it well.

CURATED CONTENT (CONTENT WITHDRAWALS)

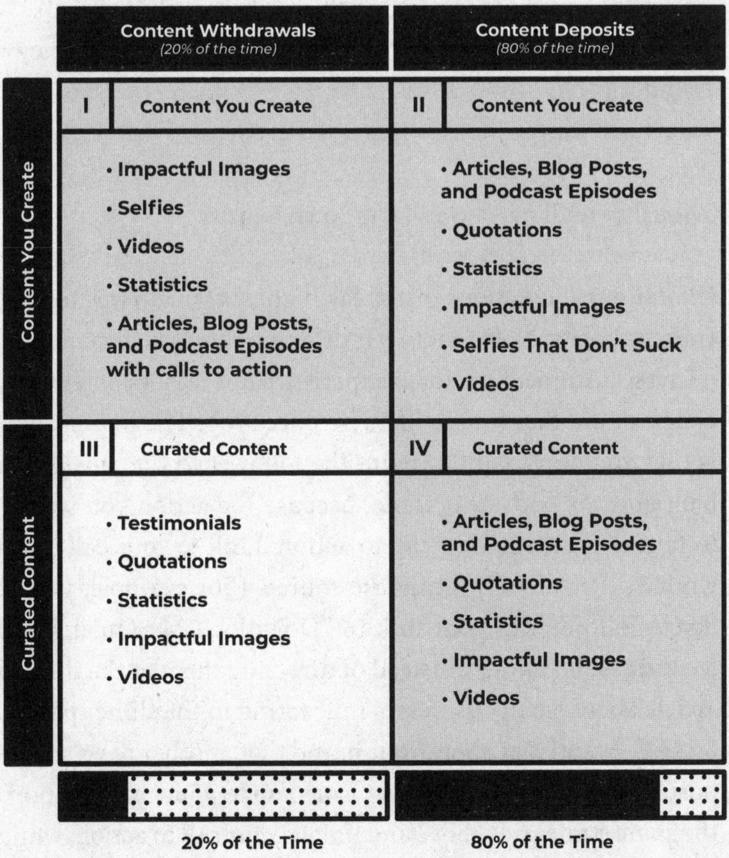

Content Withdrawals *(20% of the time)*		Content Deposits *(80% of the time)*	
I Content You Create		**II** Content You Create	
• **Impactful Images** • **Selfies** • **Videos** • **Statistics** • **Articles, Blog Posts, and Podcast Episodes with calls to action**		• **Articles, Blog Posts, and Podcast Episodes** • **Quotations** • **Statistics** • **Impactful Images** • **Selfies That Don't Suck** • **Videos**	
III Curated Content		**IV** Curated Content	
• **Testimonials** • **Quotations** • **Statistics** • **Impactful Images** • **Videos**		• **Articles, Blog Posts, and Podcast Episodes** • **Quotations** • **Statistics** • **Impactful Images** • **Videos**	

Content You Create / Curated Content (left vertical labels)

20% of the Time | **80% of the Time**

The best way to get people at the cocktail party to hear about your awesome widget is for someone else to talk about how great it is. On social media the same thing applies. Once someone else warms up your follower by talking about your greatness, you can add in a call to action to close the story gap. When it comes to curating content that closes the story gap, here are some ways to do that:

- *Testimonials*: Testimonials from happy customers are a great way to introduce a call to action. Great testimonials help brands to "showcase your value, the results you get for your customer, and the experience people had working with you."[8] Use this simple formula when advising customers on how to write a great testimonial for you:
  - Part 1: I had this problem, and here's how I felt (i.e., bad).
  - Part 2: The brand solved my problem, and here's how they did it.
  - Part 3: Now my life is better, and here's how I feel (i.e., good).

Obviously, you'll need to use your own words!

- *Quotations*: Quotations that speak highly of you do well to establish your authority. Note that this is different than a testimonial in that it isn't a customer's personal experience but rather content from an article or another source that references you. The important thing is that you don't want to point the follower to the outside article, blog post, or podcast episode, because the action you want them to take this time is *your* call to action. Link to your call to action, while still accurately citing the source. (For example, you would direct followers to your link to "Download My Quick Guide to Making Neon Slime!" instead of directing them to the third-party article about small businesses innovating in the slime space.)
- *Statistics*: Statistics about your brand that another news source has posted can also help a follower warm up to your call to action. Use the same strategy as above and link to *your* call to action, while still citing the outside source.

- *Impactful images*: Powerful curated images from others that lead up to your call to action are a great idea.
- *Videos*: A video you curate as a lead-up to a call to action of your own also can work well.

CONTENT YOU CREATE TO WITHDRAW

Content Withdrawals (20% of the time)		Content Deposits (80% of the time)	
I Content You Create		**II** Content You Create	
• Impactful Images • Selfies • Videos • Statistics • Articles, Blog Posts, and Podcast Episodes with calls to action		• Articles, Blog Posts, and Podcast Episodes • Quotations • Statistics • Impactful Images • Selfies That Don't Suck • Videos	
III Curated Content		**IV** Curated Content	
• Testimonials • Quotations • Statistics • Impactful Images • Videos		• Articles, Blog Posts, and Podcast Episodes • Quotations • Statistics • Impactful Images • Videos	
20% of the Time		80% of the Time	

This is the most direct type of social media content you can share that will close the story gap to move someone up your engagement ladder.

In your BrandScript you likely wrote out only one or two of your most powerful direct and transitional calls to action. Since you don't want to blast the same calls to action all the time, you will need to come up with many more versions of these calls to action for social media to avoid constant repetition. That's because a website homepage or sales newsletter subject line only happens once, whereas social media happens all day!

The easy way to create more versions of your direct and transitional calls to action is to use different types of original content you have created to introduce them.

Here are some examples:

- *Impactful images*: Powerful images of your own can deliver great value and lead up to a call to action.
- *Selfies*: Selfies can be a fun way to lead up to a call to action.
- *Videos*: Videos are a highly engaged form of social media that perform well as a call to action lead-up.
- *Statistics*: If your brand has great proprietary statistics that can help you with a direct or transitional call to action, go for it.
- *Articles, blog posts, and podcast episodes*: As long as these created pieces of content include clear calls to action, this is a great way to invite your social media followers to respond. A regular blog post about what you did today, though, isn't an example of a call to action. But a sales page or a podcast episode devoted to selling your new coaching package is.

Ultimately, your social media bank accounts need both deposits and withdrawals to keep them balanced and to grow them over time. Just remember the difference between a piece of content that deposits value and one that withdraws. Are you selling something? It's a withdrawal. Are you closing the story gap in any way by inviting someone to your call to take action? It's a withdrawal. Deposits and withdrawals are both needed, but it's important to know what you're posting in order to keep your social media budget in balance.

Additionally, remember that each brand's social media budget will include different content envelopes. Understanding what content works for your character is all about your BrandScript.

Content Withdrawals (20% of the time)		Content Deposits (80% of the time)	
I Content You Create		**II** Content You Create	
Content You Create	• Impactful Images • Selfies • Videos • Statistics • Articles, Blog Posts, and Podcast Episodes with calls to action		• Articles, Blog Posts, and Podcast Episodes • Quotations • Statistics • Impactful Images • Selfies That Don't Suck • Videos
III Curated Content		**IV** Curated Content	
Curated Content	• Testimonials • Quotations • Statistics • Impactful Images • Videos		• Articles, Blog Posts, and Podcast Episodes • Quotations • Statistics • Impactful Images • Videos
20% of the Time		80% of the Time	

Now that we've looked at the *story* in the SHARE model, it's time to move onto the logistics of *how* to SHARE.

The SHARE Model for Social Media Success for Every Brand

STORY

Use your StoryBrand BrandScript on social media to open the story gap, move your followers up an engagement ladder, and close the story gap when you call them to take action.

Remember:

- The first step in the SHARE model is *story*. Content is queen, and the content for your social media marketing comes from your StoryBrand BrandScript.
- Social media marketing is usually *brand marketing*, not *direct marketing*. That means that most of the time your goal is not an immediate sale.
- Effective social media marketing should always *open the story gap*, move followers up an *engagement ladder*, and then *close the story gap* with a *call to action*.
- Your *social media bank account* only thrives with give-and-take. Remember the 80/20 rule. Deposit value 80 percent of the time by opening the story gap with your content. Then, 20 percent of the time make a withdrawal by closing the story gap with a call to action.
- To balance your *social media budget*, vary the types of content you deposit and withdraw. Content should come from different content envelopes, including things like curated content, original content, articles, quotations, statistics, testimonials, direct calls to action, transitional calls to action, impactful images, selfies, video, etc.

If you learn better by video, access a free five-video minicourse at SocialMediaMadeSimple.com.

CHAPTER 3

HOW: WHO'S THE KING OF YOUR SOCIAL MEDIA ACCOUNT?

Don't Make It Too Hard to Start

In 2012, I spent the better part of a year working with the team at the Vatican to onboard Pope Benedict to Twitter, and *Wired* magazine eventually called me "The Woman Who Got the Pope on Twitter." In the years since, the number one question I get about this experience is: Does he really do his own tweeting?

Spoiler alert: Yes and no.

At Twitter I spent years onboarding high-profile individuals to the platform. The Pope, Warren Buffet, actors, musicians, CEOs, politicians, and philanthropists all shared the fact that their time was limited and taking on one more thing was not high on their list. Could someone on their team just do the tweeting for them?

I remember sitting with Sally Osberg, then-CEO of the Skoll Foundation, over lunch one day in the UK as she posted her first tweets. She was excited but concerned. Where would she find time in her busy day to keep it up?

First, I told her about Arianna Huffington. Huffington had once told me that posting to Twitter was an easy thing to fit into the margins of her day while she waited for meetings to start or while riding as a passenger in the car.

Then I told her about Obama.

When President Obama won the election in 2008, his campaign had garnered 5 million social media followers, a huge number in the pre-Kardashian days.[1] Here are some of the breakdowns of what that looked like on the various social networks:

By November 2008, Obama had approximately 2.5 million (some sources say 3.2 million) Facebook supporters, outperforming McCain by nearly four times. Obama had more than 115,000 followers on Twitter—more than twenty-three times those of McCain. Fifty million viewers spent 14 million hours watching campaign-related videos on YouTube, which was four times McCain's viewers.[2]

When he was elected, his followers received one final message: "All of this happened because of you. Thanks, Barack."[3]

Ultimately, it was widely accepted that "a major success factor for Obama's victory was how Obama's campaign used social media and technology as an integral part of its strategy, to raise money, and, more importantly, to develop a groundswell of empowered volunteers who felt they could make a difference."[4]

Given all this, you would expect he was personally doing much of his own tweeting.

You would be wrong.

Most notably, in a speech in 2009 he said, "I have never used Twitter."[5]

It wasn't until January 2010, a full fifteen months after winning the election as the first US president to truly embrace social media, that President Obama pushed the button on his first tweet. He was visiting the American Red Cross following the devastating earthquake in Haiti and sent out a tweet from the American Red Cross account.[6]

 @RedCross

President Obama pushed the button on the last tweet. It was his first ever tweet!

Even after that, though, it would take another year for him to start tweeting (occasionally) on his own. In 2011, President Obama and Twitter cofounder Jack Dorsey held a Twitter town hall at the White House. It featured President Obama answering questions that came in via Twitter using the hashtag #AskObama during a streamed event online and then sending a sample tweet from @whitehouse.[7]

 @whitehouse

BREAKING: 1st Twitter @townhall w/ Pres Obama at the WH on 7/6 @ 2ET. #AskObama your Qs on the economy & jobs: askobama.twitter.com

And finally, it wasn't until 2015 that he sent his first tweet on his own personal account—this time poking fun at Bill Clinton.[8]

 @billclinton

Welcome to @Twitter, @POTUS! One question: Does that username stay with the office? #askingforafriend

 @POTUS44

Replying to @billclinton
Good question, @billclinton. The handle comes with the house. Know anyone interested in @FLOTUS?

Ultimately, the fact that Obama's messages on social media were generally written and posted by his campaign staff for so many years did not detract from his power on social media.

Spoiler alert: this is true of *many* high-profile individuals. Although some actors, businesspeople, and politicians like Arianna Huffington or President Trump may do their own posting, others rely on a team to manage their social media. For the most part followers don't know the difference.

In the case of Pope Benedict, after he clicked "tweet" on the iPad in the televised launch event in December 2012, his staff took over. Most of the tweets during his tenure were direct quotes from his weekly homilies.

It is easy for brands to get hung up on the "who" as a means to putting off getting started. Everyone wants the perfect social media strategy, and many brands think that must start with the perfect person creating the posts. Although it may be ideal to have a CEO or founder personally post their social media messages and interact with their followers, that is often not the reality.

A great brand should have a social media manager or team who can take on the task of representing the personality of the brand and the founder when needed and following up with fans, making sure people are heard and appreciated.

Don't let perfect be the enemy of good.

HOW MANY ACCOUNTS DOES YOUR BRAND NEED ON EACH PLATFORM?

Most brands have multiple products, divisions, or initiatives they want to talk about in their social media marketing. That's why so many brands these days face the question of how many different social media accounts they should create. Should every initiative have a separate account? How specific should one get? Should you divide and conquer? Or consolidate and win?

First, take the Social Media Brand Evaluation to determine your social media priority platforms (see appendix 2).

Then remember that your brand should only ever consider multiple accounts within one platform (several different Facebook accounts for different areas of your business, for example) on your *priority* platforms.

Generally speaking, multiple accounts within one platform can get messy—fast. For some businesses, this strategy of dividing up their efforts can quickly snowball into dozens of Twitter, Instagram, or Facebook accounts all targeted to different products or divisions. This is a headache and a half, and from a branding perspective it's almost always way more trouble than it's worth.

Take the experience of Tsh Oxenreider, a bestselling author and podcaster who runs a business focused on simplicity. Like many brands, she initially created different accounts to represent the different sides of her business. Then, she felt the backlash. Ultimately, she decided to stop posting on the Instagram account dedicated to her podcast and instead redirect all her efforts to her main Instagram account.[9]

As she explained to her followers:[10]

@thesimpleshow

In some ways, it's been fun to watch this Simple Show IG account grow, mostly to hear your thoughts and reactions to episode drops! But in smaller, more acute ways, I've learned that trying to divide and conquer for the sake of Being Everywhere is the opposite of how I like to steer my ship. I'm all about fewer but better. I mean, SUPER all about it... It's the best way for me to live my life and run my work.

And so, while I'll keep this IG account live (mostly so people can tag it when they want), I'll be reminding you of new SS episodes only on my personal account from now on @tshoxenreider, specifically in my Stories. And I'll be cultivating community over in Patreon, where I'd love for you to join for more connection with me at patreon.com/tsh (and where I've got a new, patron-only show for you!). As always, subscribing to SS is the BEST way you'll never miss an episode, so make sure and do that wherever you listen to podcasts.

And as always, here's to doing things the way that works for YOU, no matter what They™ say. It's a good place to be, and it's where I always want to stay. I'm so grateful for each of you! ♥

Importantly, the downside of dividing your efforts isn't just an emotional one. It's also about practical social media engagement success. The reality is that there are often algorithmic benefits to growth when you consolidate your social media efforts. Algorithms vary by platform and are constantly changing, but typically the more followers you have on an account the more likely your content will be seen. This means that you'll have a better chance of reaching more people if the bulk of your followers are consuming and engaging with your content in one place. Other ancillary benefits exist as well. On some platforms, for example, you need a minimum number of followers to get verification.

All this to say, should you have multiple accounts for different products or divisions?

My rule of thumb is that whenever you can keep things on one account, do.

WHEN TO POST ON SOCIAL MEDIA

If you craft a great social media post, you want to make sure it gets the attention it deserves. That said, it can be hard to know when the right time is to post.

When it comes to the best time of day and the best day of the week to post on social media, the key is to know your audience. The same goes for considering a big sales promotion; it is important to know the right months of the year that work for your industry. Different audiences have incredibly different behaviors when it comes to when and how they use digital media.

Let's look at a few examples.

If you run a nonprofit organization, you know that December is likely your biggest month of the year to solicit donations and that January is a ghost town. In contrast, if you are in the health and fitness industry you know that January is when all the magic happens. A breast pump manufacturer targeting new moms on maternity leave might get its most engaged activity on social media during afternoon naptime hours or after bedtime on weekdays. A meditation app that targets busy executives might find that the early morning slot before the work day starts on weekdays is best.

And it's not always intuitive. A church pastor might think her worshippers are turning off technology on the Sabbath, but find out that Sundays are the time when her motivational quotes are most likely to spread. I sell an online productivity course that teaches real people with real lives to finally become productive. I always see a huge uptick in customers to my Work by Design products in January, which makes sense, but I also see interest in the end of August. I believe that so many of my customers juggle both work and school-age kids that they see the fall as a second New Year. Finally, no two brands within the same industry are the same. Back to the car example: Tesla buyers and Volvo buyers may both be in search of a new car, but chances are their lists of needs and their lifestyles are vastly different. Do those weird doors have child safety locks? #askingforafriend

Knowing your audience is so important that it's better to figure it out for yourself over time than to listen the experts.

Claire Pelletreau is a Facebook ads expert who helps small businesses. Several years ago, she discovered that both engagement with her social media content and the sales of her course, Absolute FB Ads, were at their highest on Sundays and Mondays. She *guessed* that was because people wanted to start their week off on the right foot, but to be honest she wasn't really sure. And ultimately it didn't really matter. Whatever the reason, the evidence was so overwhelming that she decided to show the ads for that course only on Sundays and Mondays.[11]

The best thing you can do is to try different times of the day and days of the week to evaluate over time what works for your followers. To start, take your best guess of when you think your followers might be most engaged and schedule posts to go out at those times. Then, dig into your analytics and test. Most third-party tools that post your content offer great analytics. (More on this coming up.)

Additionally, remember that if you plan to schedule social media on several different platforms, you will see different behavior. This makes sense if you simply think about how you yourself use platforms differently.

If you're a corporate employee, you might be more likely to read LinkedIn during the day and retreat to Facebook at home after work. If you're an entertainment blogger, you might be frequently posting and commenting on Instagram during the weekdays but use Twitter to live-tweet your favorite TV shows at night.

TOOLS TO USE FOR POSTING

Although it is certainly possible to independently post your social media updates within the individual native platforms, many brands find it easiest to use a third-party management tool to help them manage all of their social media platforms at once. Let's look at a few of the most popular tools out there.

Hootsuite. This tool has been around since the early days, and it's the first third-party tool I used to manage my social media accounts. It is arguably the most well-known of all management options and offers plans for businesses of all sizes. It's an all-around good choice. Hootsuite also does a great job allowing for comment moderation within the system, something that not all tools offer.

Buffer. The great benefit of a tool like Buffer is that you can put all your planned posts into one content bucket, and then the system parses out the content automatically into the schedules you preset for each individual platform. Even when you are planning to post the same content on several social media platforms, Buffer will stagger the schedule, so the posts go out at different times. Remember that one drawback of tools like Buffer is that they are not set up for comment moderation. Thus, when you want to engage with those commenting on your posts, you should go directly to the platforms themselves.

Sprout Social. This is a more robust tool popular with small businesses aiming to scale. It has a higher price point, which comes with key benefits. Sprout Social sets itself apart by helping your brand grow with more advanced discovery options, helping you find people to connect with in your industry. It also offers great analytics reporting.[12]

Sendible. Sendible is most popular with agencies who manage multiple accounts.[13] They have smaller plan options available for solopreneurs and small businesses, but their strength is servicing companies with multiple brands and many accounts.

Remember that all of these tools can help with the curation process. You can add in the relevant blogs in your niche and they will automatically show you the latest posts, so you can easily share them. This helps you avoid scouring the web every time you want to curate something.

Whichever tool you use, make sure it works for you and your team.

THE IMPORTANCE OF REGULARITY

One of the best ways to make sure your followers don't forget about you on social media is to keep delivering content on a regular basis. (As we'll explore, your specific posting schedule will vary.)

At the most basic level, this means that it's not a good idea to leave your social media followers in the lurch by disappearing on them for days at a time. In the same way that you open up your local newspaper or online news app every morning, your followers want to be able to turn to you with regularity to know what's going on in your world. No matter what the schedule is, keeping it regular allows them to count on you.

An ongoing feature can also be a good way to expand upon this practice.

Years before live video, charity: water, a nonprofit organization, had a regular "photo of the day" feature on Twitter where they posted one wonderful image of their work in the field on a daily basis. This worked from a few different perspectives. For followers, it gave them something to look forward to every day. For @charitywater, it was highly engaging evergreen content they could schedule out far in advance. The concept was so popular that other accounts followed their lead.

These days, many social media followers think of live video in a similar way.

When I was a kid, TGIF came on every Friday night at 8:00 p.m. on ABC. Coming home from school on Friday afternoon, I always looked forward to Urkel's latest antics on *Family Matters*. Social media works in the same way. These days, I know that life coach Mary Hyatt (who I'll tell you more about later) comes out with her inspirational YouTube Live show every Wednesday at 1:00 p.m. central standard time. Women like me can plan for it, look forward to it, and tune in.

YOUR SOCIAL MEDIA SCHEDULE AND YOUR SOCIAL MEDIA EDITORIAL CALENDAR

With all of this in mind, now's the time to come up with a social media calendar for each of your priority social media accounts. (Take the Social Media Brand Evaluation in appendix 2 to determine your priority platforms.)

A social media calendar will allow you to schedule posts in advance and know when it's time for spontaneous posting. It will also ensure that you are balancing out your social media budget on each priority account with the different types of content deposits and withdrawals to keep followers highly engaged and keep your social media bank account in the black.

Here are a few examples of potential calendars that could work depending on your specific priority social media platforms:

EXAMPLE
I · Social Media Marketing Schedule

		Light User	Moderate User	Heavy User
#1	Priority platform: **Facebook**	10 times a week	Twice daily	Three times a day on weekdays; twice a day on weekends.
#2	Platform: **Twitter**	5 times a week	Once daily	Once daily
#3	Platform: **Instagram**	Not a priority	Several times a month	Five times a week
#4	Platform: **LinkedIn**	Not a priority	Not a priority	Twice a week

Keep in mind that your usage (heavy user, moderate user, light user) is entirely dependent on your brand's bandwidth. If you have a full-time social media manager, you will be able to take on significantly more posting than a one-woman-shop. Think about what you can realistically commit to.

Remember the 80/20 rule. You want 80 percent of the content to be a deposit that opens the story gap. Then 20 percent of the content is a withdrawal that closes the story gap and brings your follower onto or up the engagement ladder with a call to action.

For example, the social media schedule and bank account of a moderate user might look like this:

EXAMPLE
- **Social Media Marketing Schedule**
- **Social Media Bank Account**

		Moderate User
#1	Priority platform: **Facebook**	**Schedule:** Twice daily **Social Media Bank Account:** Of the fourteen posts a week, ten are deposits and four are withdrawals
#2	Platform: **Twitter**	**Schedule:** Once daily **Social Media Bank Account:** Of the seven weekly posts, five are deposits and two are withdrawals
#3	Platform: **Instagram**	**Schedule:** Several posts a month **Social Media Bank Account:** Two to three deposits and one withdrawal
#4	Platform: **LinkedIn**	**Not a priority**

Then you'd look at your social media budget to determine how these withdrawals and deposits break down in terms of your different content envelopes.

This is all about your BrandScript.

Let's say based on the character in your BrandScript that you decide your main content envelopes will be curated articles, quotations, images, and videos. (Selfies and statistics aren't relevant to your brand, you decide.)

If you decide to divide these more or less evenly between the four content envelopes, your social media budget might look like this:

EXAMPLE
- **Social Media Marketing Schedule**
- **Social Media Bank Account**
- **Social Media Budget**

		Moderate User
#1 Priority platform: **Facebook**		**Schedule:** Twice daily **Social Media Bank Account:** Of the fourteen posts a week, ten are deposits and four are withdrawals **Social Media Budget:** Two to three deposits each of curated articles, quotations, images, and videos
#2 Platform: **Twitter**		**Schedule:** Once daily **Social Media Bank Account:** Of the seven weekly posts, five are deposits and two are withdrawals **Social Media Budget:** One or two deposits each of curated articles, quotations, images, and videos
#3 Platform: **Instagram**		**Schedule:** Several posts a month **Social Media Bank Account:** Two to three deposits and one withdrawal **Social Media Budget:** One deposit each of a quotation, image, or video *(Curated articles aren't as much of a thing on Instagram)*
#4 Platform: **LinkedIn**		**Not a priority**

When it comes to your withdrawals, remember that those are direct calls to action or transitional calls to action to close the story gap and move people up the engagement ladder. How you format these withdrawals—in a video, a testimonial, a selfie, or an image—should also vary to some extent, although your main goal is to figure out what type of calls to action work best with your followers and use those more often over time.

For example, if I try a few formats of calls to action and realize that my followers respond best to selfies and testimonials, then my schedule could look like this:

EXAMPLE
- **Social Media Marketing Schedule**
- **Social Media Bank Account**
- **Social Media Budget**
- **Social Media Deposits and Withdrawls**

	Moderate User

#1 Priority platform: **Facebook**	**Schedule:** Twice daily
	Social Media Bank Account: Of the fourteen posts a week, ten are deposits and four are withdrawals
	Social Media Budget
	   Deposits: Two to three deposits each of curated articles, quotations, images, and videos
	   Withdrawals: Two selfies, two testimonials

#2 Platform: **Twitter**	**Schedule:** Once daily
	Social Media Bank Account: Of the seven weekly posts, five are deposits and two are withdrawals
	Social Media Budget
	   Deposits: One to two deposits each of curated articles, quotations, images, and videos
	   Withdrawals: One selfie, one testimonial

#3 Platform: **Instagram**	**Schedule:** Several posts a month
	Social Media Bank Account: Two to three deposits and one withdrawal
	Social Media Budget
	   Deposits: One deposit each of a quotation, image, or video *(Curated articles aren't as much of a thing on Instagram)*
	   Withdrawal: One post a month of either a selfie or a testimonial

#4 Platform: **LinkedIn**	**Not a priority**

Planning out the exact posts that will go in these slots (and allowing some breathing room for spontaneous posting) will be the next step. This is called building your *social media editorial calendar*.

Remember that you will be using similar versions of content on all platforms. For example, if you post a great article on Facebook, you would also post it to Twitter. With or without the same headline.

You will make changes over time as you get more information about what works and what doesn't for your followers. We'll look at how analytics can help you with this later, but in summary, over time you may see that you need to try different content developments, and you may need to try a different breakdown of your budgets.

Continuing with our above example, let's say based on the character in your BrandScript that you decide your main content envelopes for your social media budget on Facebook, your priority platform, are curated articles, quotations, images, and videos. (You initially think selfies and statistics aren't relevant to your brand.) One day, however, you are surprised to see a competitor using a selfie and getting some great responses. You decide to try it for yourself, and the analytics show that it does get great engagement with your followers. This conclusion might mean it's time to try selfies as a new content envelope—either in addition to the other four envelopes you already have or as a replacement for an existing one that doesn't seem to be working well. (You aren't getting many clicks on any of your curated articles, after all.)

By the same token, let's say you initially decided to divide your social media budget equally among your various content envelopes. When you see that images do so well, though, you decide to make this content envelope take up a larger share of your posting.

This is the type of tweaking you will do over time.

Finally, remember that you will see differences from platform to platform. In the same example, in the social media budget for your priority social media platform, Facebook, you decided your content envelopes were curated articles, quotations, images, and videos. On Instagram, your second priority social media platform, articles aren't user-friendly. So on Instagram your social media budget could break down differently into these content envelopes: quotations, images, and videos.

Setting up your marketing schedule and editorial calendar for your priority platforms is a lot of work, but the wonderful thing is that once you have it up and running, you can maintain it with far less work than you likely spend on your social media posting today. Most importantly, you'll finally have a social media marketing system that sells.

THE KINGS OF MARKETING KNOW HOW TO USE PATTERN DISRUPTION

Ten years ago, when my husband and I were first dating, and I still ate gluten, there was a bakery called Bell'Aria that played a key role in our lives here in Buenos Aires. The croissants were to die for, and I knew a certain someone named Claire who would buy a dozen in the morning and then come back later in the afternoon for a dozen more.

Bell'Aria's marketing, however, left something to be desired. In fact, we used to laugh that they were "The Kings of Marketing" for what we deemed to be a marketing promotion that could only have been developed by an insane person.

Here's how the promotion worked:

It was called "Bell'Aria Hour" (it sounds better in Spanish), and the idea was that at totally random times during the week there was a sixty-minute period wherein all customers would get an extra box of croissants with their purchase. There was no rhyme or reason to the schedule, and walking in the door, you never knew whether or not the free croissants would rain down.

This is crazy! We'd laugh. *How is this effective marketing?! You never know when it's going to be!* And then we'd scurry back to the shop for more, on the off chance we might be lucky.

Recently, we were reminiscing about Bell'Aria and their insane marketing promotion.

"The thing is, they really did have the best croissants in the city," my husband said. "Yeah, and the whole promotional hour really did make us go back a lot . . ."

We looked at each other sheepishly. Were the Kings of Marketing really insane marketing geniuses?

I'll let you be the judge.

When it comes to social media, regularity only gets you halfway to the finish line. Doing something unplanned and creating a pattern disruption is also critical to keeping followers on their toes. In this day and age, we are so interested in unexpected happenings online that sometimes it seems that 90 percent of all celebrity-related headlines (not a verified number) have to do with a celebrity doing something unexpected on social media (unfollowing someone they are supposedly married to, deleting their account, posting a scandalously naked bathroom selfie, etc.).

Instagram Live video is a great example of this.

We spend almost an hour a day on Instagram, and one of the reasons is live video.[14]

Depending on the number of people you follow and the amount of time you spend on the platform, when you log onto Instagram to view the latest images and stories, you are also likely to see that someone you follow is also live at that very moment. This increases the time you spend on that platform and makes it more likely that you'll come back soon to repeat the cycle. That's good for Instagram, good for the person you follow, and good for you (providing it is valuable content).

This also works for other types of content.

Bestselling author Jen Hatmaker is known for her random tweet-storms of both highbrow and lowbrow television experiences. She'll get on a tear and won't get off until her followers are rolling on the floor, as she did when discussing Olympian swimmer Ryan Lochte's hair during her Rio Olympics live-tweeting:[15]

 @jenhatmaker

I went to my prayer closet over Ryan's hair. I lit a candle & interceded. Fix it, Jesus. Give us strength. Give a light unto our path. #Rio

 @krby0404

Replying to @jenhatmaker
Jen, I seriously can't with your Rio commentary. Im just sitting at my desk snickering. Please never stop tweeting the Olympics

 @jen4redemption

Replying to @jenhatmaker
I can't even! #fixitjesus

It may not be live video, but it is just as effective in increasing the time her followers stay on Twitter and in making it more likely that they'll come back for more Jen, more of the time. Good for Twitter, good for Jen, and good for her followers.

Now if only Jen could tweet me some flaky croissants.

POST LESS OFTEN, TAKE A SOCIAL MEDIA BREAK, CHANGE YOUR PLATFORM OF CHOICE, OR DECLARE SOCIAL MEDIA BANKRUPTCY

Pattern disruption can be so effective that it can make posting less often work to your advantage.

Although social media followers in general don't respond well to the complete disappearance of someone they follow when it's for no particular reason, life happens. When I gave birth to premature twins and spent almost two months hanging out with them in the hospital, social media was understandably not my top priority.

The result?

Whenever I did post, my engagement was through the roof. Like when I posted this after weeks offline.[16]

Purposely going offline for a period of time can have a similar effect.

Some years ago, I felt my Twitter life was getting out of control. At one point I thought that following less than one hundred people was a good rule of thumb for me. My rationale was that at this number I could realistically know what my followers are doing. Over the years my resolve had softened, and I was following more than seven

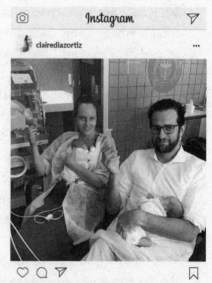

Instagram

clairediazortiz

♡ ◯ ⦥ 🔖

162 likes

clairediazortiz Mateo and Santi are one month young today! Getting big and strong and loving the ease with which the magic of feeding tubes delivers effort-free milk to their big bellies. Who wants to suction?! This is the life! (For NICU junkies, this is known as a "double gravity feed"...to which Jose asked, "really? so them growing depends on...gravity??")

hundred smart, lame, hysterical, annoying people. I tried to edit my list down. I'd unfollow ten people and then feel FOMO and follow them all over again. I clearly needed to do something more drastic, especially when I realized that I was ignoring my main timeline. So I did. In one fell swoop, I unfollowed everyone and declared Twitter bankruptcy.

The result was beneficial in a variety of ways.

First, it made me excited about Twitter again. After a couple days of following no one, I began to see things with new eyes. I reminded myself of all the awesome people and accounts that were right in front of me, and I made sure to add those back into my life. It also helped me stand out to some of my followers who had forgotten about me because of the seven hundred other people *they* follow. I did something jarring and newsworthy and they took notice. Finally, it convinced me of the power of more regular break-taking. For me, and for my followers.

Last year I took a complete twenty-one-day digital detox. No email, no internet, no social media. It was a great experience on a personal level, but it once again proved useful for my social media following. The posts I made when I came back online were some of my most engaged posts in ages. The reason? I had shaken things up by going offline, and then had shaken them up again by coming back on.

Mary Hyatt saw the same thing when she switched her social media platform of choice. She used to have a popular Instagram account sharing inspiration with women. When she quit Instagram and Facebook and stopped posting entirely on those platforms, her followers took notice. Thankfully for us, she didn't go away completely. Instead, she decided to move her online activity to YouTube. We went with her, more eager than ever because she'd made us hungry for content in her absence.

Another gold star for the power of shaking things up. At the end of the day, using social media well doesn't require you to hardwire yourself into one platform day in and day out. With the SHARE model, *how* you win is with strategy and spontaneity in equal measure.

The SHARE Model for Social Media Success for Every Brand

HOW

Learn the practical logistics of *how* to post your content.

Remember:
- Take the *Social Media Brand Evaluation* to determine your brand's priority social media platforms (see appendix 2). Concentrate on the platforms that matter most to your brand.
- To decide how many accounts you need on each platform, remember that the fewer accounts you have, the better.
- Who posts matters less than you think. When to post matters more. Time of day, day of the week, and season of the year are all considerations.
- Third-party tools can help with scheduling, curating, and analytics. Hootsuite, Buffer, Sprout Social, and Sendible are all good platforms that offer different benefits.
- Consistency is important. Ensure that you create a *social media schedule* and *social media editorial calendar* that work for your audience and your brand's bandwidth.
- Use pattern disruption and selective break-taking to your advantage.

If you learn better by video, access a free five-video minicourse at SocialMediaMadeSimple.com.

CHAPTER 4

AUDIENCE: SOCIAL MEDIA— IT'S NOT ABOUT YOU

In a world of perfectly filtered selfies and instant gratification on every post, it's easy to think that social media is about you.

Newsflash: Your brand is not the hero. Your customer is.

Let's revisit the basics of the StoryBrand process to remind us why. The SB7 Framework relies on two principal characters: the hero and the guide. The guide's role is to lead the hero on a transformational journey to solve his or her problem using a clear plan. When brands learn the StoryBrand process, they usually do a double take when they hear who the hero of the story really is.

On social media, the same is true. Your company's account is not the hero. Your follower is. (After all, your social media followers are your existing or potential customers.)

This doesn't mean that your brand can't talk about itself. What it does mean is that it is important to make your story about your audience and to always seek ways to increase empathy and connection along the way, rather than constantly post about your own awesomeness. (Hello cocktail party dude everyone hates.)

Brands who understand this are the ones who are wildly successful on social media. Even when they *are* sharing selfies.

THE MAGIC EQUATION ON SOCIAL MEDIA

I may hate math, but I love social media. That's why I know this equation like the back of my hand.

Here's how it works:

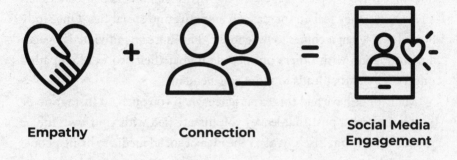

Empathy   **Connection**   **Social Media Engagement**

Empathy is historically defined as "the projection of one's own personality into the personality of another in order to understand him better."[1] And a key way to create empathy is to tell a story that draws in your audience and builds a bond. As P. J. Manney says, "Storytelling is both the seductive siren and the safe haven that encourages the connection."[2] Brené Brown adds, "Empathy is at the heart of connection."[3]

For your brand to get followers to feel connected with you on social media, you need to generate empathy. And this leads to the engagement (and the engagement ladder) that you seek.

Studies show that empathy has dropped significantly in the last generation, and many theorize that it is directly related to the passive use of social media and the tendency to isolate online while you "compare and despair" over someone else's perfectly curated social media feed.[4]

One such study can be found in the *Journal of Evolution and Technology*, where P. J. Manney explains: "As the world grows smaller and more connected, the role of empathy grows larger and more important than ever. . . . However, as our technological connectedness has increased, there does not appear to be a proportionate increase in global empathy. Instead, we are living in a time of relatively decreasing empathy, compared to our connectedness to the greater world."[5]

While the researchers are right, they are leaving out one important factor: engagement. It turns out that much of this disconnection comes from the passive use of social media, not the engaged use of it.[6] Studies show that when people engage *actively* with social media platforms such as Facebook, they feel an increase in empathy and social ties. One study showed that when it comes to Facebook, "The more an individual engages in conversation with others online, the higher their scores of empathic concern."[7] And that leads to more engagement.

Many of us have had this experience when you open up Instagram or Twitter and see a post that leaves you dissatisfied with your own life or envious of someone else's. Wasn't the idea of social media to bring people together? If social media is supposed to be about connection, how do we keep it from pulling us apart?

Ultimately, people open social media aiming to find engagement. If they get it, they come back for more.

THREE WAYS TO GENERATE THE EMPATHY YOUR AUDIENCE WANTS

Let's look at three ways that you effectively create empathy: tell a great story, help someone, and ask a question.

TELL A GREAT STORY

The first step in making your story about your follower is to figure out who that is. Once you do, find out how to speak to them. Remember that when creating your StoryBrand BrandScript we called this defining your character and figuring out what they want on an internal, external, and philosophical level. This is a high-stakes endeavor. "When we fail to define something our customer wants, we fail to open a story gap. When we don't open a story gap in our customers' mind, they have no motivation to engage us."[8]

Let's look at an example.

Hard Exercise Works is a high-intensity fitness center based in Florida with dozens of locations throughout the US. They told me they were concerned that their marketing message was directed more toward athletes and not toward the real people who worked out in their gym— the moms, dads, firefighters, dog walkers, and babysitters who make up the bulk of their membership. We used the StoryBrand process to create a BrandScript to guide them in rebranding.

Here's what we came up with:

The Character: An everyday client. (Not an athlete!)
The External Problem: A client wants to get in shape.
The Internal Problem: A client doesn't know where to start and doesn't believe in her own ability to stick to a plan and do the hard work to make the change.
The Philosophical Problem: Changing your life shouldn't be so hard.
The Tag Line: "We help you do the hard work to get the body you want."

I then began to dig into their existing online material to find great video testimonials. I immediately saw a problem. Much of their existing video content focused on stories about intense challenges that their accomplished members had taken. These were exactly the type of thing that could scare off someone who's just getting up the nerve to walk in the door.

And then I found a video they had recorded of women in their gym reacting to a *New York Times* article stating that, scientifically speaking, women could not do a pull-up.[9] A series of real women who were gym members could and did, narrating the whole way. It was exactly the way for this company to speak to their audience going forward.

DON'T POST AND GHOST

Remember that making your story about your audience is an on-going, real-time process. Don't post and ghost.

Public speakers are familiar with the phrase "read the room," which indicates that understanding the responses of your participants to the story you are telling is critical. This is all about real-time feedback. On social media, you get that through engagement. If you put up a powerful post and then don't check your Facebook page for a week, you won't be very effective. It's important to learn what resonates and over time narrow in even more on exactly what your followers respond to.

HELP SOMEONE

Another key way to create empathy on social media is to help someone.

You don't have to do a fund-raiser for a great cause or stage an elaborate activism campaign. Helping someone can simply be solving a problem.

There are a variety of ways of doing this, and sometimes the easiest way is to simply answer a question someone else has. When I was thinking of changing my daughter to a new school, I asked my followers how far they thought it was reasonable to commute.[10,11]

 @claire

What is the acceptable commute time for a child's school? (seriously. answer!)

 @jennaworthen

Replying to @claire
I think you can spend 30 quality minutes in the car together before you hate yourself.

@tsh

Replying to @claire
We drive 40 min one way for our special needs kiddo's school.
But it's also only 3 days a week.

 @tsh

Replying to @claire
I get it. I'll say that after 2.5 years of doing the drive, we're used
to it. It's my time with the kids (we often do a big audiobook),
then on the solo drive back I catch up on my podcasts. Kinda
nice, really.

 @nishweiseth

I think it depends! I've got a special-needs kiddo, so I'd
probably go further than most for better services.

At the end of the day, I got good answers that helped inform my decision and also bonded me with my followers—some of whom are readers of my books.

BE WILDLY USEFUL

Another easy way to help your audience is to pass on important resources. You see many brands doing this in times of crisis. You don't have to be a weather channel to alert your followers about the emergency numbers for an upcoming storm in your local area. Show that you care and want to provide support in any way you can.

SERVE THE LOW-HANGING FRUIT

On the side of customer service, there are many opportunities to use social media to directly reach out and solve a problem someone has

---

with your business. Brands often have a stream of incoming questions or concerns about their product or service. One of the easiest ways to help on social media is to address this low-hanging fruit.

Importantly, making sure your social media presence is really about your audience also involves proactively going out and looking for people talking about you.

One day, Danielle Brigida, acting deputy director of digital strategy at the US Department of the Interior, who was then managing social media for the National Wildlife Federation, found a customer tweeting about not being able to subscribe online to the organization's magazine. Now keep in mind they weren't tweeting at the organization directly; they were just tweeting *about* it.

 @NWF

Dear National Wildlife Federation, I would happily renew my kids magazine subscriptions if your site worked.

Brigida immediately stepped in, solved the problem, and moved one more happy customer up the engagement ladder.

National Wildlife Federation magazine resubscribe success! :) Great magazines for kids. http://ow.ly/1tema

ASK QUESTIONS

You can also build empathy and connection on social media by asking a question. This works equally well for accounts with lots of followers and ones that are just starting out.

People love providing their opinion and feeling that their voice has been heard. Giving them the chance to do this by lobbying a question into the social media ether is a great step.

Leila Janah is a social entrepreneur and the founder of both Samasource—a nonprofit organization that gives work to those who need it most—and LXMI, a sustainable for-profit beauty brand. On social media she always emphasizes her commitment to sustainability. Since her work requires her to travel more than two hundred thousand miles a year, she recently took to her Instagram feed to ask her followers about what *they* do to offset their carbon footprint.[12]

She got dozens of well-thought-out responses from her followers, who encouraged her to try different strategies or research relevant tools and organizations while also providing a valuable, on-brand resource to those followers. Leila kept the conversation going in the comments section to continue the engagement, something that her followers will remember the next time she asks a question.

Asking questions on a regular basis can be a great way to create ongoing engagement. For more than five years, Scott Williams, a pastor in Oklahoma City, used to have a popular meme on Twitter on Sundays. It was simple and effective. All he did was ask people where they were going to church.[13]

◎　　　𝓘𝓷𝓼𝓽𝓪𝓰𝓻𝓪𝓶　　　▽

🅿 leilajanah　　　　　　　　　...

The top ways to reduce your carbon footprint

Emissions savings (tons of carbon dioxide equivalents)

Have one fewer child

Live car-free

Avoid one round-trip
trans-Atlantic flight

Buy green energy

Buy a more efficient car

Switch from an electric
car to car-free

Eat a plant-based diet

Replace gasoline with hybrid

Wash clothes in cold water

Recycle

Hang-dry clothes

Upgrade light bulbs

CREDITS: (GRAPHIC) J. YOU/*SCIENCE*; (DATA) SETH WYNES
AND KIMBERLY A NICHOLAS, *ENVIRONMENTAL RESEARCH
LETTERS* (2017)

♡　♁　▽　　　　　　　🔖

435 likes

leilajanah Have been thinking about my personal carbon footprint and researching organizations that offset carbon emissions from flights (at a cost of ~$15-18 per ton...200k miles in a year is just under 40 tons) by investing in reforestation and other kinds ofcarbon sequestration. Eventually this should just be part of the taxes we pay to fly...but for now, check out goldstandard. org — and please share any tips you find for responsible traveling. (Also...check out this chart!)

 **@scottwilliams**

Where will you be attending church today? Name, Location, Pastor, Twitter Handle... use #ChurchRollCall hashtag

The responses always came flooding in, and he would respond in turn to those who answered.

This also works well when speaking directly to someone on a 1:1 level to deepen the engagement. Southwest Airlines does this in their customer service tweets. To the delight and chagrin of many, this low-cost North American carrier eschews assigned seats. Instead, you are assigned a boarding number in the order of when you check in. Then, you race to snag your seat when you get on the plane. When someone is lucky enough to have the very first boarding number—A01—they often turn to social media to express their pleasure.

Southwest Airlines regularly reads their tweet stream for folks in just such an unusual state of airline-related bliss. Not only do they respond but they ask a further question to continue the conversation and create another positive moment.[14]

 @fox_trot35

When you randomly get picked for the A-team aka boarding spot for @SouthwestAir 😍

 @southwestair

Replying to @fox_trot35
With your pick of seats ahead of you, where are you going to sit? Back row, middle? Bulkhead, window? So many choices. Enjoy the ride, Caroline! -Adam

 @vumander

Look who hit the @SouthwestAir check in lottery

 @southwestair

Replying to @vumander
It's like seeing a unicorn. We're getting a little emotional over here. So, where are you going to sit? -Adam

Question-asking is so effective on social media that there are entire platforms built just for this purpose. (In chapter 11, we'll dive into how brands can effectively use these.)

Following the divisive 2016 presidential election, the marketing team at Florida's Natural orange juice teamed up with Funny or Die to take question-asking to the next level. They created their own debate on Facebook Live. "Pulp, No Pulp, or Some Pulp" featured three candidates (Pulp, No Pulp, and Some Pulp) campaigning for the hearts of America. They did three live debates total, generating more than half a million views.[15]

Asking questions from your personal accounts to remind others about your brand is also useful.

Jess Gaertner of the Modern Mamas Podcast took to her personal Instagram account to ask her followers a question that also helped remind them about the podcast she records under a different name:[16]

jess.holdthespace   •••

78 likes

jess.holdthespace If you had a podcast what would you name it?? Naming our podcast (The Modern Mamas Podcast) was actually the EASIEST part of the whole setup process believe it or not! Laura said "what do you think about this name?" and I said "I love it, let's do it." and that was that!

If you could host your own podcast (which btw you totally can) what would it be called and what would it be about?! I want to hear all the fun ideas I know are out there in your creative heads!

You can also create goodwill by asking questions that might seem like they don't directly benefit your brand. For more than seven years, the Balanced Bites podcast has brought weekly listeners valuable information on health and nutrition. But they don't make it only about them. The @balancedbitespodcast recently asked their followers what other podcasts folks listen to, giving us all some valuable information.[17]

Finally, remember that creating engagement with empathy and connection does not mean you have to always be on message. As mentioned earlier, at times it is okay to go off-script from your BrandScript (we'll talk more about this later). When I asked my followers how far they'd commute to take their kid to school, I did so not because I'm in the chauffeur business but because I'm in the connection business.

The SHARE Model for Social Media Success for Every Brand

AUDIENCE

Your social media marketing should be about your *audience*, not your brand.

Remember:
- Your brand is not your hero; your customer is.
- Your customer (or potential customer) is your follower. Reframe your social media account to make it about them.

- Cultivating empathy on social media matters to building a relationship with your customers and reaching long-term success. Remember this equation: Empathy + Connection = Social Media Engagement.
- Generate empathy (and engagement) by telling a great story, helping someone, and asking questions.
- Don't post and ghost. Great social media marketing requires real-time connection and engagement with your audience.

If you learn better by video, access a free five-video minicourse at SocialMediaMadeSimple.com.

CHAPTER 5

REACH: INCREASE YOUR REACH TO AMPLIFY YOUR BRAND

Crafting a Social Media Profile That Opens the Story Gap

It turns out that if you want advice on how to craft a great social media profile for your brand, you should never look at the profiles of any of the founders of a social media platform.

Here's why.

Jack Dorsey is arguably the most important person on Twitter. He cofounded the platform and serves as its CEO. His Twitter bio does not point to anything along those lines, however. What it does indicate is anyone's guess. Unlike any brand trying to amplify their message, he gives us no idea who he is or how he can help us be the hero of our story.[1]

Mark Zuckerberg does marginally better. As probably the most important person on Facebook, he works hard to not tell us this. His intro, "Bringing the world closer together," is clear as mud, but things become even more confusing when he indicates he "works" at the Chan Zuckerberg Institute—surely a great place but not his most well-known position.[2]

jack ✔
@jack

Joined March 2006

Mark Zuck

Timeline

③ Intro

Bringing the world closer together.

Founder and CEO at Facebook
Works at Chan Zuckerberg Initiative
Studied Computer science at Harvard University
Lives in Palo Alto, California
From Dobbs Ferry, New York
Followed by 118,154,419 people

Here's the thing: you are not Jack or Mark, and your brand is not Twitter or Facebook. If you are looking to amplify your brand's message on social media, then you want people to understand what your business is and how it can help them.

The easiest way to do this is to use your StoryBrand one-liner in your profile content. This ensures that your social media profile opens the story gap in the same way that your social media content does.

When Don Miller first launched StoryBrand, he used this very tactic on his Twitter profile to land his first client. He didn't have much of a business yet when he added a few simple words to his profile about how he had started to help brands develop their brand story. Followers took notice, and he drew interest from a company that would become StoryBrand's first client.

That company? Procter & Gamble.

These days, in the text of Don's bio on Twitter, he clearly states the problem his followers and potential followers face and how he can help: "Most companies struggle to talk about what they offer but if you confuse, you'll lose. My framework helps you clarify your message, so customers place orders."

The hero image on his profile further drives the point home, along with a well-designed header bearing the message: "I help companies clarify their message, so companies engage. Don Miller, CEO, StoryBrand."[3]

On Facebook, the header of the StoryBrand page is equally clear:[4]

The About section on Facebook goes in deeper with the backstory while still staying clear and succinct.

All social media platforms are not the same, and what works on one profile may not work on another, even in the same industry. Additionally, your brand's content may vary widely from one platform to another.

For example, let's say you are a dental practice and you take the Social Media Brand Evaluation (see appendix 2). You find out that your priority platform is LinkedIn, followed by Twitter and Facebook. Instagram is your lowest priority and will understandably not get much attention. That said, you would like to snag your username, put up a complete profile, and occasionally post for fun.

You decide that a fun way to use your Instagram is to post behind-the-scenes photos of the office cat a few times a month, and you write your profile to reflect that. This keeps followers from expecting announcements on upcoming teeth-whitening promotions on Instagram and encourages them to follow you elsewhere for that engagement.

Your example Instagram profile could read: "I provide quality dental care that doesn't scare children. Find me on LinkedIn at [URL]. Here, I mostly post photos of our ugly office cat."

WHO MATTERS MORE: YOUR NEW FOLLOWERS OR YOUR OLD ONES?

The number one question I get from brands about social media is, "How can we get more followers?"

Unfortunately, this is the wrong question.

In 2011, I was working at Twitter when some research analysts at the company discovered what they thought was an anomaly in the data when researching tweets.[5] Over and over, they saw that tweets about Bible verses and inspirational religious quotes were getting crazy engagement. Some further digging proved what no one at first believed: religious content had incredibly high engagement and religious leaders punched above their weight in terms of follower count. (As an example, a religious leader with one thousand followers might get way more engagement than a celebrity with one hundred thousand.) Soon thereafter, part of my role at Twitter shifted to targeting high-profile religious leaders in the same way that we were already going after Hollywood celebrities. When we succeeded in getting Pope Benedict to join Twitter and he immediately became the most-followed user on the platform across all his accounts (and had great engagement to boot), it was clear it had worked.

What most brands do not understand is that the success of your reach on social media is far less dependent on new follower growth than it is on how engaged your existing followers are with your product or service. Thus, the number one question a brand should have about social media, even more than acquiring new followers, is: "How can we move followers up the engagement ladder?" There are endless examples of accounts with large followings that get less engagement than accounts that are a fraction of the same size.

Is there a point at which follower count can trump anything? Maybe, but I'm not convinced. For evidence, refer to the introduction and the sad marketing story of Rob Kardashian and his socks.

HOW TO GET NEW FOLLOWERS

Your current followers are the most important, but understandably growth is still an objective for your brand. So how do you get new followers?

There are three basic ways:

1. Create great content.
2. Use influencer marketing.
3. Pay for social media advertising to boost either of the above strategies.

Let's explore how these strategies work.

CREATE GREAT CONTENT: WHY GREAT CONTENT LEADS TO NEW FOLLOWERS

Some years back, I sat in author and comedian Jon Acuff's office asking him what was working for him on Twitter. He said he had undertaken an experiment to try to respond to everyone who wrote him publicly on Twitter. Over a series of months, he believed this had doubled his followers. Jon didn't have hard numbers. But I believed him.

Here's why.

Great content combined with increased engagement among existing followers makes *any* content you create more likely to spread. It doesn't matter how many times Facebook or Twitter or Instagram or LinkedIn change their algorithms; this one thing will always be true. Social media platforms want to reward engaged accounts, because those are the accounts that make their world sing (and earn the social media companies their money). The more engaged your followers are on any platform, the more favorable any algorithm will be to show more of your posts to more people, more often.

This also explains another mystery. Have you ever wondered why a promoted post you saw on Facebook doesn't lead you to an offer but rather to a blog post on a website the ad wants you to read? Why is someone paying for you to read a random article and not go to a sales page? After all, you could just find the article for free yourself! Here's the answer: the ad is banking on the fact that by creating any engagement with you in the form of a click on an article link, you will be more likely to open future social media posts from that account (hello algorithm!) and be more likely to move up their engagement ladder to further engagement.

GREAT HASHTAGS PUT GREAT CONTENT ON STEROIDS

Carolyn Rivers Mitchell is the circus manager for Club Med in Ixtapa, Mexico, and one of only a handful of women in the world who can claim this title. As I can attest, she can make even the most uncoordinated among us achieve a knee hang.

When she was in college at the University of Virginia, she took a class on social media marketing that challenged students to get one hundred new followers in one week on a brand-new Instagram account. She was already an aerialist at the time, so it was natural for her to choose to start an account about the circus arts.

Although her curated circus content soon went far beyond one hundred followers, the account only began to get big when she started using a new hashtag she had come up with. These days, #circusinspiration has been used almost half a million times, all thanks to Carolyn.[6]

Ultimately, the hashtag is a key tool that can extend the reach of your brand. It was initially created by a Twitter user,

Instagram

flyingcarolina

871 likes

flyingcarolina Hey y'all!!! 👋 Been a minute since I've introduced myself on here... so here goes! My name is Carolyn Rivers Mitchell, but you can call me Rivers. 🎪💫 Currently I work as a Chief of Circus (GO) for @clubmed in Mexico and I have the best. life. ever. I get to do what I love, with people I love, and travel around the world while we do it. The Dream, or what?! In the past three years, I've also lived in Florida, Turks & Caicos, and BALI You can see why the heart eyes is my favorite emoji... I think to myself EVERY day that I'm probably the luckiest girl ever. 🙋

As for circus, I'm mainly teaching and training flying trapeze 🤸 My other loves are silks and double trapeze, but I'd definitely consider myself a generalist overall (like I'm pretty good at many things but not exceptional at any in particular lol)

I created this account 4 years ago in college (shit!) with #CircusInspiration as a way to stay involved with the insta-circus community, while I was studying. I always toyed with the idea of taking it personal... & now going on 6 months, it's been so rewarding 👐 Here you can find me keeping it real with circus - building blocks, behind the scenes, & bloopers, my international adventures, & my best attempt to be a strong female role model. 💪 When I started this journey I couldn't do a pull up, I had never performed, I didn't even know how to hold kids on the trapeze. And now, well, I run the damn thing 😜

If you've read this far leave me a comment (or a DM!) and introduce yourself as well - I'd love to put an actual person behind the username!! What's your circus fav? Let's chat!! See you there 🎪

Chris Messina, who first "suggested use of the hashtag to make it easy for 'lay' users to search for content and find specific relevant updates."[7,8]

 @chrismessina

how do you feel about using # (pound) for groups. As in #barcamp [msg]?

His idea gained steam, and hashtags were first widely used during the 2007 wildfires in San Diego. Since then they have become a huge part of first Twitter and now all social media platforms.

Although anyone can use any hashtag they want and no one "owns" a hashtag like you own a social media account, certain hashtags are known for being mostly used when talking about one thing. For example, the overwhelming majority of tweets with the hashtag #49ers are going to be about the football team, not about the ukulele band you started with two of your other friends who are also pretending they aren't yet fifty. That doesn't stop you from tweeting about your band, but it does mean that given the competition you are up against, you are unlikely to build a long-term movement dedicated to your special music.

To make a great hashtag, follow these two rules:

1. Be as general as you can get away with.
2. Don't use a hashtag that most people already associate with something else.

Catalyst is a large conference company that hosts many events in various cities throughout the year. Like many conferences, they used to create a new hashtag for every single event based on the year and the city. It was incredibly hard for speakers and attendees to remember the hashtag at a given event. Speakers would be on stage encouraging the audience of thousands to tweet and then stop and say, "Wait, was the hashtag Cat2017ATL or CATATL17 this year?" Everyone regularly used the wrong hashtag, ultimately diluting its overall power. Furthermore, each hashtag was only relevant for the length of an event, which took away from its ability to build into a movement over time.

I advised Brad Lomenick, then head of Catalyst, to get rid of all the confusion and centralize his message in one great hashtag: #catalyst.

In the case of Catalyst, they had a brand name that was unique enough that when I searched for instances of other people using the hashtag, I didn't find a ton of tweets about something else. This won't work if your desired hashtag is something super general like #health, or if it is something already overwhelmingly associated with something else, like #49ers.

YOU DON'T USUALLY HEAR OF AN ANGRY METHODIST

Methodists aren't known for their rabble-rousing, but hashtags may be one key to changing all that.

In the summer of 2018, the government of the Republic of the Philippines subjected three young United Methodist missionaries to false accusations and delayed their exit from the country for months. Adam Shaw and Miracle Osman were first detained for a few hours, then released but prohibited from leaving the country. Tawanda Chandiwana was detained by the government for eight weeks and spent several of those weeks in confinement at a detention camp.

The missionaries, citizens of the US, Zimbabwe, and Malawi respectively, came under surveillance when they took part in an international fact-finding mission of alleged human rights violations on the island of Mindanao, which was under martial law. The missionaries and United Methodist leaders in the Philippines denied any wrongdoing, and Manila-based attorneys for the three tried to negotiate their release with the authorities.

When legal efforts were met with delay after delay, the United Methodist Church reacted swiftly, appealing publicly to the Philippine government to release them.

Thomas Kemper, general secretary of the General Board of Global Ministries of the United Methodist Church, which is the denomination's worldwide mission and development agency, stated toward the end of June, "We have exhausted all our diplomatic and church channels. . . . Nothing has come to fruition."[9]

The church's next step was to add a digital component to their diplomatic strategy.

On June 26, Kemper released a video via email, social media, and YouTube asking supporters to sign an online petition to release the missionaries. The petition served as a vehicle to draw public attention to the missionaries' plight, enable people from all walks of life to play a role in the protest, and show other missionaries that the public supported them. In the video, Kemper called out the name of a hashtag-ready movement—Let Them Leave—and encouraged viewers to sign the petition at the website and to share it using the hashtag #LetThemLeave.

Marcy Heinz, senior communications manager, says the effort was coordinated across multiple agencies within the United Methodist Church and partner agencies.[10]

Within four days, the petition had surpassed its initial goal of ten thousand signatures.[11]

 @umcmission

Words cannot express our gratitude to the more than 10,000 people who have signed the #LetThemLeave

petition. We're not done yet. Continue to share and sign!
#TawandaKasamaMoKami

At a press conference in Manila, local advocates pressured the government and shared the preliminary results of the petition drive.

Since the missionaries weren't home yet, the church kept at it.[12]

 @umcmission

General Secretary Thomas Kemper takes a moment to
thank the National Council of Churches in the Philippines
for asking the government to let our three missionaries
Tawanda, Miracle and Adam leave. Show your support by
signing our petition today. #LetThemLeave @NCCPhils

They knew that supporters wanted to be involved as things changed, so real-time updates were important in increasing support over time.[13]

 @kemper_t

Just left the detention centre in Manila after my visit with
Tawanda. #letthemleave it was great to have some hours
with him, pray and enjoy the company of this incredible
young #umc missionary.

Amazingly, by July 13, 2018, all three missionaries had been allowed to leave the Philippines.

Heinz says the #LetThemLeave hashtag strategy worked because it drove widespread visibility through social media posts, vlogs (video blogs), blog posts, and news articles. Starting in the Methodist church circles, it then expanded to the Philippine news media, and then took on a life of its own when it hit mainstream international news sources, making it all the way to the *New York Times*. All told, the online petition garnered signatures from 18,530 people from over 110 countries.[14]

Heinz emphasized that "usually this story wouldn't get traction," but the story-driven nature of the hashtag strategy, the many players involved, and the frequent Twitter and Facebook updates were fundamental to its success.[15,16]

 @umcmission

Tawanda Chandiwana and Miracle Osman share a special thanks to the more than 18,500 people who signed the #LetThemLeave petition. Your participation made it possible for our missionaries to depart the Philippines safely. Thank you! #UMCMission @umcmissiongt

globalministries
Adam Shaw, a Global Ministries missionary in the Philippines who was denied permission to leave the country this summer, takes a moment to express his gratitude for the thoughts and prayers of those who supported him during the #LetThemLeave campaign.

In a world that sometimes criticizes social media for its ineffective activism (slacker activism, or "slacktivism" is a favorite disparaging phrase), this campaign stands out. Heinz cuts to the chase: "We measured success by the clearest metric. Were they allowed to leave?"

They were.

I used to have trouble convincing people about the long-term power of hashtags to create movements that go well beyond social media. After all, not everyone had heard of campaigns like #LetThemLeave, #icebucketchallenge, #bringbackourgirls, or #givingtuesday.[17]

All that has changed in recent years. First, there was #BlackLivesMatter. As the *Chicago Tribune* said, "For those eager to criticize hashtag activism, the Internet raises you #BlackLivesMatter. Used 12 million times, the hashtag has quite literally transformed from an online-community unifier to a political movement and tangible organization."[18]

And then there was #MeToo. Even though the #MeToo movement was started in 2006 by Tarana Burke, people are so familiar with it as a hashtag that most think it started when actress Alyssa Milano first used it in a tweet in 2018.[19]

 @alyssa_milano

If you've been sexually harassed or assaulted write 'me too' as a reply to this tweet.

At the time Milano didn't even know about Burke's use of #MeToo. Since then the two have collaborated. On Twitter alone, more than 19 million tweets used the hashtag in its first year. When you count all the other social media platforms (like Facebook and Instagram) that #MeToo appeared on, and the many different-language versions of it in other countries, the true number of uses is significantly higher.[20]

USE INFLUENCER MARKETING: WHY INFLUENCER MARKETING GROWS YOUR SOCIAL MEDIA FOLLOWING

In 1995, if you wanted to get in touch with a celebrity, you didn't have many options.

You could drive out to Beverly Hills, find a guy standing on a street corner, pay $9.99 for a map of celebrity houses, and go knocking door-to-door. Maybe you'd have luck, and someone famous would be sipping a martini on their front porch right when you knocked. Alternatively, you could go to your local library and check out a book called something like *Real Celebrity Addresses* and send out a bunch of letters with fifty-five-cent stamps. Finally, you could try firing up your external modem and logging onto Altavista to find a list of phone numbers of famous Hollywood agents to try calling.

None of these options were that reliable. But this was the world before social media.

When Twitter launched in 2006, it was the first time you could directly contact anyone you wanted. As long as they had a Twitter account, they were contactable. You didn't need to be friends with them or be connected with them like on other social media platforms. You could technically write them. And people did.

Over the years, some of the best stories I have heard about brands using Twitter, and now other social media platforms, relate to how businesses connected with influencers and built supportive, long-term relationships that benefit their brands.

My favorite example comes from Global Citizen Year.

Global Citizen Year is a nonprofit organization pioneering a model that wraps education and instruction around real-world experience to transform the trajectory of our most promising young leaders. As I describe in *Twitter for Good*, Global Citizen Year's CEO, Abby Falik, didn't become a big fan of Twitter until she realized how useful it could be for finding and develop relationships with influencers. In her case, developing a relationship with *New York Times* journalist Nick Kristof made all the difference.[21]

As Falik told me, "I've always been a huge admirer of Nick Kristof, and the ways he uses his skill and influence to shine a massive spotlight on critical global issues that would otherwise go unseen. . . . At the same time, he has been a vocal advocate for the 'gap year' as a unique opportunity for young people to see the world beyond our borders. Knowing his personal interests were so closely aligned with our mission at Global Citizen Year, I reached out—initially via Twitter!—to enlist him as an ally."

Falik's organic attempts to make an early ally of Nick Kristof highlight some key best practices about reaching out to influencers on social media. When she first began to test the waters of Twitter, she used the @GlobalCitizenYr Twitter account to reference articles that Kristof had written on relevant topics to her own followers. Not savvy to Twitter yet, she wasn't even initially using his Twitter handle when she talked about him.[22]

 @GlobalCitizenYr

"some time at the grassroots is an invaluable addition to classroom learning"- Kristof - http://ping.fm/ZlqpY

She soon found his account on Twitter, followed him, and began sending public @replies to his then–Twitter handle, @nytimeskristof:[23]

 @GlobalCitizenYr

@nytimeskristof & let's make it before college when young people are still forming their senses of themselves in the world - Global Citi ...

As time went on, Global Citizen Year retweeted relevant tweets from Kristof, including an article he wrote supporting one student's gap year in the Congo.[24]

 @GlobalCitizenYr

RT @nytimeskristof: More young Americans should spend time in the dev world. Here's the blog of H. McConnell, in Congo: http://bit.ly/3nbNJM

After reading his book *Half the Sky*, in which he also encourages gap years, Global Citizen Year wrote a blog post in response.[25]

 @GlobalCitizenYr

Kristof voices support for bridge year in "Half the Sky." Read a few excerpts on our blog - http://bit.ly/4Kaola

Kristof began to notice the organization's outreach and started to retweet their tweets from his new account @NickKristof. Then he praised them directly:[26]

 @GlobalCitizenYr

RT @NickKristof: Impressive effort to give young people a gap year to learn about the world, get skills to save it: http://bit.ly/7JIdZZ

The current communications and technology manager, Wil Keenan, said that a thousand people clicked to read about Global Citizen Year from that tweet. Months later, Kristof wrote about Global Citizen Year in the *New York Times*. The organization tweeted it widely:[27]

 @GlobalCitizenYr

Kristof cites GCY as he stresses the need 4 Americans
2 embed in other cultures - it's a national priority
http://nyti.ms/aUhmOT

Global Citizen Year didn't stop there, and they worked hard to make the most of this publicity win. Gaya Morris, a fellow in the field in Senegal, wrote a blog post responding to Kristof's article. Global Citizen Year then sent it out on Twitter, including Kristof in the tweet.[28]

 @GlobalCitizenYr

Fellow, Gaya Morris responds to @NickKristof in her post
discussing education & the teacher shortage in Senegal
http://bit.ly/90Dxi1

Kristof responded in turn, also promoting the blog post.[29]

 @NickKristof

An American student teaching in Senegal responds to my
"Teach for the World" proposal: http://bit.ly/90Dxi1

From then on, every time he tweeted about them, Global Citizen Year retweeted the tweets to increase their own authority and highlight the powerful testimonial to their followers.[30]

 @GlobalCitizenYr

RT @NickKristof: An American student teaching in
Senegal responds to my "Teach for the World" proposal:
http://bit.ly/90Dxi1

The interactions on social media continued, and the relationship blossomed. Global Citizen Year kept referencing Kristof:[31]

 @GlobalCitizenYr

@nickkristof: Every child on earth could get a primary ed for the cost of 5 wks military spend in Afghanistan: http://nyti.ms/brlloV

Kristof continued to talk about the organization:[32]

 @NickKristof

Sage advice from a young American on her gap year in Senegal: http://bit.ly/9X4HMy

And Global Citizen Year showed their appreciation. On social media, this has the added effect of serving as a public testimonial and increasing the organization's authority.[33]

 @GlobalCitizenYr

A must-read post by Fellow, Tess Langan RT @NickKristof: Sage advice from a young American on her gap year in Senegal: http://bit.ly/9X4HMy

A year after Global Citizen Year and Kristof began to connect on Twitter, alumni Tess Langan wrote an article in the *New York Times* about why she put off Colgate College for a gap year in Senegal:[34]

 @GlobalCitizenYr

Fellow, @TessLangan in her piece in the @nytimes "I am spending my year in Senegal. College will have to wait." http://nyti.ms/9p1dH7

In the years since, Kristof has consistently continued to cheer on the organization, and the relationship of support has extended beyond social media. These days, the Global Citizen Year brand has greatly expanded, and this early push by such a prominent journalist played a role. As Kristof said, "I always hear from young people who want to go abroad but think it's unaffordable or too dangerous, or their parents are aghast at the idea. So when I heard of an organization working to address those concerns, backed by someone with Abby's credentials, I wanted to help spread the word."

Importantly, he added that this wasn't the first time: "Something similar happened with Givology, by the way. I think I found out about them elsewhere, but then I became aware of their Twitter presence and followed them. That led to occasionally retweeting them or highlighting their work. And following them certainly put them more on my front burner than they ever would be otherwise."[35]

SUCCESSFUL INFLUENCER OUTREACH LOOKS LIKE THIS

Many brands would love an influencer marketing success story like Global Citizen Year's. Thankfully it's not as hard to replicate as you might think.

The first step is identifying the exact influencers or the type of influencer you are trying to reach. In the case of Abby Falik and Global Citizen Year, this was an organic process in that she already knew Kristof's work. In the case of your brand, you may have some people in mind, but it also may require some research.

Here are some steps to getting started:

Find the niche. First things first, start following the key groups and hashtags in your niche. On LinkedIn, look for influencers and private groups. On Twitter and Instagram, look for hashtags. On Facebook, look for public pages or private groups.

Find the influencers. This is fairly straightforward. Find potential influencers in your space by looking for the accounts in a given niche that are creating a lot of valuable content, getting a lot of engagement, and have a healthy number of followers. (They don't need to have massive amounts of followers, but newbie accounts are likely not very influential.) Some of the social media marketing engagement tools discussed in chapter 5 can help.

Then, start following some of these accounts. Most importantly, narrow it down to go after people who may be a "reach" for your brand but are not an impossibility. For example, if you run a nonprofit serving adoptive parents, go for an engaged blogger in the adoption space, not Oprah. While reaching Oprah would be cool, the chance you have of reaching her and that she could help is less likely.

Stay organized with your outreach by not going after too many people at once. On Twitter, for example, you can create a private list of target influencers. This allows you to remember to check in a few times a week by responding, retweeting, or mentioning someone you want to pursue. On other platforms the mechanics work differently.

Start engaging. Now it's time to start engaging with those influencers to try to build a conversation.

While it may be considered rude in real life, on social media one of the best ways to start talking *to* someone is to first talk *about* someone. Influencers know who their number one fans are, especially if those individuals offer valuable content of their own.

Tag your target in your LinkedIn or Facebook post or mention them in your Instagram post or Tweet. Blog about them in a LinkedIn blog post. Retweet or reshare someone's content. After you do this a handful of times, then get more direct and start talking *at* an influencer in a public way. On Instagram, this might mean simply being a regular commenter or it might mean taking a more specific tactic like posting several comments on different images all in a row to attract attention and encourage a follow.

After you've built up credibility with this type of interaction, it's much easier to send a private message (availability of this depends on the platform and the settings of the influencer). Remember that this is a long-tail game. Going for the quick win and getting an influencer to immediately post about your work and then forget you forever is neither wise nor effective.

SIX DEGREES OF SOCIAL PROOF
ON SOCIAL MEDIA

In the SB7 Framework, social proof is a useful way to help convey your brand's authority. On social media, a positive public conversation, comment, like, or reshare acts as the "social proof" to help take an interaction with an influencer from the public realm to the private one.

For example, when author and speaker Brené Brown posts an Instagram photo of her at a football game with author Jen Hatmaker, it introduces Brené's fans to the work of Jen Hatmaker.[36]

Whether or not Jen posts on her own Instagram (she did in this case), many of Brené's fans will in turn start to follow Jen.[37]

If a new follower then sees that her longtime favorite author Shauna

Niequist is also commenting on Jen's posts, this is further social proof in the eyes of the new follower and increases her interest and likelihood of engaging with Jen, Shauna, *and* Brené. (And that's exactly why social media platforms make a point of telling you if someone you are already friends with or follow has engaged with content you are viewing.)

In terms of influencer marketing, such social proof then also applies to that follower's interactions with Brené, Jen, and Shauna and can extend to those of any of these individual influencers. For example, if one day this new follower says something to Jen in a public comment on a social media platform and Jen responds, that new follower can then reference that interaction when she makes a direct private connection with Jen (or with Brené or Shauna). Think of it like six degrees of social proof.

Ultimately, growing your social media following comes from creating great content, engaging in influencer marketing campaigns, and using paid advertising to get more eyeballs on these efforts. Unfortunately, the rise in both influencer marketing and social media advertising has meant that many brands now spend lots of money attracting new followers while not effectively serving the ones they already have. Remember that the *r* in *reach* teaches that we should never spend time focusing on new followers at the expense of our existing ones.

The SHARE Model for Social Media Success for Every Brand

REACH

To amplify your brand on social media, it's important to expand your *reach*.

Remember:
- Craft a killer social media profile that increases your authority and opens the story gap by using your BrandScript.
- Prioritize your existing social media tribe over new followers every day of the week.

- The three ways to get new followers on social media are to create great content, use influencer marketing, or pay for advertising to boost either of those strategies.
- Great hashtags can put great content on steroids. When crafting a hashtag, be as general as you can without using a term people already associate with something else.
- Concentrate on reaching influencers in a way they like. Remember that it's a long-tail game that relies on finding the right niche, finding the right influencer, and engaging with them over time.

If you learn better by video, access a free five-video minicourse at SocialMediaMadeSimple.com.

CHAPTER 6

EXCELLENCE: EXCELLING AT SOCIAL MEDIA MARKETING

How to Get Everybody to Love Your Drunken Tweet

When Buzzfeed blasts a headline that reads, "Red Cross Employee Accidentally Tweets About Getting Slizzard, People Donate Lots of $$$ to the Red Cross," statistically there's a 100 percent chance that I will click to see what happened.

One slow Friday afternoon at the American Red Cross, then–social media manager Gloria Huang accidentally tweeted the following from the main American Red Cross account, thinking it was her personal account:[1]

 @RedCross

Ryan found two more 4 bottle packs of Dogfish Head's
Midas Touch beer.... when we drink we do it right
#gettingslizzerd

The internet went wild. Would the American Red Cross—one of the most respected institutions in the country—be able to come back from such a mishap? And if so, how?

First, Gloria tweeted out an apology from her own account:[2]

 @riaglo

Rogue tweet frm @RedCross due to my inability to use
hootsuite... I wasn't actually #gettingslizzard but just
excited! #nowembarassing

Next, the main American Red Cross account sent out a tweet acknowledging what had happened to its hundreds of thousands of followers.[3]

 @RedCross

We've deleted the rogue tweet but rest assured the Red
Cross is sober and we've confiscated the keys.

As a final positive turn in an already positive story, the Dogfish Beer brand took it upon themselves to tweet out what had happened and ask followers for donations to the American Red Cross.[4]

 @DogfishBeer

RT @Michael_Hayek: #craftbeer @dogfishbeer fans, donate
2 @redcross 2day. Tweet with #gettingslizzerd. Donate here
http://tinyurl.com/5s72obb

Not only did the American Red Cross turn around a potential PR disaster with speed, grace, and humor, but they did so in a way that generated unexpected positive coverage and encouraged a bunch of donations. On blogs and news sites everywhere, the resulting story was far less about the mistake than about the handling of it. Ultimately this proved what can happen when brands use social media well—even in a PR crisis.

Unfortunately, not all brands are as adept at overcoming drunk tweeting as the American Red Cross.

THE ART OF SUCKING AT SOCIAL MEDIA

Sucking at social media is a timeless art, and many of the biggest brands around have at some point or another made a disastrous social media post destined to kill their business.

Like McDonald's. One day in March 2017, the main McDonald's account on Twitter tweeted:[5]

 @McDonaldsCorp

@RealDonaldTrump You are actually a disgusting excuse of a President and we would love to have @BarackObama back, also you have tiny hands.

In an effort to clean up the mess, McDonald's took the questionable tactic of a lot of corporate mumbo jumbo. Blaming a vague shadowy entity and citing an "investigation," they said, "we have determined that our Twitter account was hacked by an external source. We took swift action to secure it, and we apologize this tweet was sent through our corporate McDonald's account."[6]

Possible? Sure. Likely? Not so much.

Chrysler, in bids to become Detroit's least favorite car company, had their own issues when an employee managing their large account tweeted out the following bombshell after a bad morning commute:[7]

 @ChryslerAutos

I find it ironic that Detroit is known as the #motorcity and yet no one here knows how to fucking drive

Chrysler apologized robotically, saying: "Chrysler Group and its brands do not tolerate inappropriate language or behavior, and apologize to anyone who may have been offended by this communication."[8]

Even Twitter executives are not immune to such mishaps. Anthony

Noto, the then-CFO of Twitter, accidentally sent a confidential direct message about a potential acquisition as a public Tweet.[9]

 @AnthonyNoto

I still think we should buy them. He is on your schedule for Dec 15 or 16 -- we will need to sell him. i have a plan

So what can we learn from the fact that huge brands—including the social media companies themselves—have unwittingly fallen off the Twitter wagon?

When it comes to being excellent on social media, it's not how you mess up—it's how you *clean up* that matters.

WHAT TO DO WHEN PEOPLE BAD-MOUTH YOUR BRAND

Remembering the old saying that "all press is good press" can also help brands rethink what defines a crisis on social media. Take the case of Starbucks' wildly successful social media launch of the equally wildly disgusting Unicorn Frappuccino.

With a whopping seventy-six grams of sugar in the venti size (more than three times the daily recommended allowance for women), its success was undeniable.[10] As one Starbucks barista on the verge of a meltdown told *USA Today*, "I have never made so many Frappuccinos in my entire life. My hands are completely sticky. I have unicorn crap all in my hair and on my nose, I have never been so stressed out in my entire life."[11]

As one article explained, "The 'Unicorn Frappuccino' was a neon-colored, fruity concoction that transitioned from sweet to sour and got some less-than-glowing reviews. Despite having a divisive flavor, the photogenic beverage turned customers into a social media army that fueled nearly 155,000 posts on Instagram and drove major foot traffic with those clamoring to taste the magic before it sold out."[12]

And it wasn't just a hit in terms of sales. The Mobile Marketer Awards called the social media launch of the Frappuccino flavor the "Mobile Campaign of the Year" and analyzed its success. "In April, the coffee chain with 8,000 stores in the US unveiled a limited-edition drink that appears to have been designed not so much for its flavor, but to spark buzz online."[13]

Importantly, the buzz about the drink wasn't positive. It just had to *exist*. And this was exactly what the Starbucks marketing team was hoping for all along. In many ways, the funny Twitter quotes about the horrors of the Unicorn Frappuccino were even more shareable than the picture-perfect Instagram images. At the end of the day, people purchased because they wanted to be a part of a real-life movement that was created on social media. It's the essence of social media building true connection. As social media strategist Keith Keller said, "It's sort of peer-to-peer, isn't it? [Starbucks] took something that was fun and turned it into a business success."[14]

People wanted to be part of the story.[15]

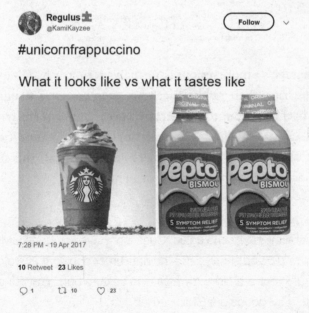

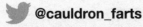 **@cauldron_farts**

my friend just sent me a pic of the unicorn frappuccino and it looks like a cupful of soap from various public restrooms

○ jonacuff ···

♡ ○ ▽   ▯

1,620 likes

jonacuff Just got my kids unicorn frappuccinos for our
10pm delayed flight to Disney that now lands at 1AM.
I don't see any possible way that this could end poorly.

But what if it's a more serious issue than a seriously bad Frappuccino? For Cheerios, their public Facebook page has long struggled with inevitable backlash from consumers because the manufacturer, General Mills, has supported legislation protecting genetically modified organisms (GMOs).[16] Many of their customers staunchly reject this stance and are vocal about their opposition on social media.

Dennis Jefferson to Cheerios
Hi General mills... It's me again. Question: Have you gone GMO
free yet or did you simply lie to the consumer hoping that we'd buy
and forget your promise? It was a nice gesture but... Still not gon
buy until your goods are GMO verified

Molly OBrien to Cheerios
I'm a Cheerios fan, but was sad to read that "General Mills has
spent over a million dollars in the past two years blocking GMO

labeling laws." Could that be right? Even if you're pro-GMO, shouldn't people have the right to know what's in their food?

As any PR expert knows, brands need to be aware that when you make a potentially controversial decision like this, not everyone will like it. And in an age of social media, you'll hear a lot about it.

Heck, on social media not everyone will like it even when you're trying to be nice.

One year on New Year's Eve, Volkswagen had the idea to innocuously ask their fans on Facebook what their brand's New Year's resolution should be. They didn't foresee that they were opening themselves up to a barrage of negativity. One user took the opportunity to detail all the problems they saw with Volkswagen's environmental policies:[17]

> Volkswagon UK
> We hope you had a fantastic New Year. Do you have any resolutions and what would you like to see us do more of this year?

In the past, it wasn't so easy for consumers to complain, and when we did it was often in a vacuum. When I was twelve, there was no social media. So when I got upset at the lip moisturizer Carmex because someone at summer camp told me it was addictive, I had to buy a stamp to alert them to my woes. In my letter, I accused them of creating a product I couldn't put down. It moisturized my lips in the short term, but the long-term result was that I was more and more dependent on their product. They wrote me back. And gave me a free tube! If I were twelve today, I can just imagine how many other enraged twelve-year-olds at summer camp I would've rounded up to tweet accusatory things at Carmex about our increasingly dry lips.

Ultimately, social media has given us all an easy, free tool to say whatever we want all day long. And sometimes your customers will do just that. If the comments aren't offensive, let the dialogue take place, and don't delete the negative content. Be authentic and transparent in your response. And whenever you can, try to turn a negative conversation into a positive one.

Remember how Danielle Brigida of the National Wildlife Federation helped a disgruntled customer happily renew their magazine subscription?

National Wildlife Federation magazine resubscribe success! :) Great magazines for kids. http://ow.ly/1tema

That's a perfect example of excellence in social media marketing. And one can only hope she gave them some free lip glop.

The SHARE Model for Social Media Success for Every Brand

EXCELLENCE

Fine-tune your social media marketing efforts to reach long-term *excellence*.

Remember:
- Always ask yourself how you can get followers to want in on your story.
- The real-time nature of social media means that you don't always know what's going to happen. Make that a good thing.
- On social media, it's about rolling with the punches. If your brand makes a social media mistake, own up to it. Fast.
- Social media gives your customers a public place to share their grievances. Sometimes they will do just that. If the comments aren't offensive, let the dialogue take place, and don't delete the negative content. Whenever you can, try to turn a negative conversation into a positive one.

If you learn better by video, access a free five-video minicourse at SocialMediaMadeSimple.com.

IMPLEMENTING THE SHARE MODEL FOR YOUR BRAND

CHAPTER 7

FACEBOOK

Last year I went to Facebook headquarters in Palo Alto. While there, I went on a biking excursion, ate a lot of gourmet ramen, and bought an overpriced piece of wooden art from a Facebook-sponsored local artisan. And then I met a Facebook employee who told me point-blank, "No one on my team actually uses Facebook."

I wasn't as surprised as you might think.

The reality is that Facebook is bearing the brunt of a lot of backlash against social media noise these days, and many people have resorted to giving up on their personal profile. But that doesn't mean it's dead for brands. Given that 96 percent of *businesses* use Facebook, it's important to get onboard and it's time to do it well.[1]

Although we think of Facebook as a first-mover in the social media network space, it was anything but.

First, there was LiveJournal. Then there was Friendster, the social networking site that *Inc.* magazine famously called "One of the biggest disappointments in Internet history."[2] Then there was MySpace. (Cue sad violins.) And then, and only then, there was Facebook.

In 2009, Facebook became the world's most used social network.[3] Ten years later, with 2.2 billion users and 1.4 billion daily active users, it has managed to stay that way. Sixty-six percent of Facebook users are on every day, and 51 percent of users visit multiple times. The average user spends more than twenty minutes on it daily. Amazingly, 91 percent of all millennials use Facebook.[4]

In this chapter, we'll explore how to use the SHARE model to win on Facebook.

THE IMPORTANCE OF STORY WHEN IT COMES TO THE FACEBOOK ALGORITHM (*S* IS FOR STORY)

There has long been a saying that "Facebook is for people you know; Twitter is for people you don't." With the frequent algorithm changes at Facebook, that has never been truer than it is right now.

We know that effective social media marketing should open the story gap, move followers up the engagement ladder, and then close the story gap when calling followers to take action. Doing this on Facebook requires understanding enough about the Facebook algorithm to beat it at its own game.

Crystal Paine runs *Money Saving Mom*, one of the top personal finance blogs on the internet. As such, she has almost one million people on her Facebook page.[5] But, due to algorithm changes, even she recently encouraged her followers to join her private Facebook group to ensure they saw her posts.

Is she onto something?

Yes. And many brands have followed suit. It turns out that creating a private group is just one of a series of tactics that can help you beat the algorithm blues.[6]

Here's what you need to know about the Facebook algorithm and why it (keeps) changing everything on Facebook.

In 2018, Mark Zuckerberg made a surprising announcement:

One of our big focus areas for 2018 is making sure the time we all spend on Facebook is time well spent. We built Facebook to help people stay connected and bring us closer together with the people that matter to us. . . . Based on this, we're making a major change to how we build Facebook. . . . The first changes you'll see will be in News Feed, where you can expect to see more from your friends, family and groups. As we roll this out, you'll see less public content like posts from businesses, brands, and media. . . . Now, I want to be clear: by making these changes, I expect the time people spend on Facebook and some measures of engagement will go down. But I also expect the time you do spend on Facebook will be more valuable. And if we do the right thing, I believe that will be good for our community and our business over the long term too.

You could practically hear businesses everywhere panicking (or, if you didn't hear them, you could just read the nasty comments on Zuckerberg's Facebook post).[7]

Translation? If you don't interact with content in your News Feed, Facebook's algorithm will show you less of that content over time. With the changes, the current priorities for what Facebook will show you in your News Feed are related to

If the content is shared over Facebook Messenger.
If the content is liked or commented on.
If the content receives multiple replies.
If the content is part of a "meaningful interaction" between users.[8]

Given that as early as 2016 a study already showed that only 10 percent of News Feed stories were read daily, you can pretty much bank on the fact that without some serious interaction your brand's posts are not going to be showing up in someone's News Feed.[9] Never mind the fact that users on Facebook are the least engaged of any major social media network, even when they do see the posts.[10]

That means that it's more important than ever to remember that content is queen and that opening the story gap for your followers to encourage them to engage is more important than ever.

HOW TO BEAT THE ALGORITHM TO BOOST YOUR BRAND ON FACEBOOK (*H* IS FOR HOW)

Once you know you have great content in the form of a story, here are some super practical ways to help your posts go far:

- Post less, curate less, and be more selective about what you post. The old days of posting ten times a day on Facebook are gone for most brands.
- Remind fans to go to the Pages Feed on the left sidebar of their News Feed to see content from pages like yours that they've liked.
- Tell your super fans to update their notification settings to see more from your page.
- Encourage fans to engage with your content to see more of your posts.
- Share videos. "According to a recent study by quintly, native Facebook videos have an 186 percent higher engagement rate and are shared over 1,000 percent more than videos linked to from other hosting sites."[11]
- Broadcast on Facebook Live: statistics show users spend three times as long on a live video as a recorded one.
- Encourage your fans to join your group to ensure they'll see your content more often.

USE FACEBOOK MESSENGER AND FACEBOOK MESSENGER BOTS FOR BUSINESS

THE RISE OF FACEBOOK MESSENGER

Alfred Lua from the social media management company Buffer argues that, "Instead of being a one-to-many channel, social media is becoming a one-to-few—and often one-to-one—channel."[12] One of the ways that is most evident is in the rise of 1:1 communication on social media platforms, like Facebook Messenger. At least 1.3 billion people now use Facebook Messenger each month. In general terms, studies show that more than 50 percent of users are more likely to shop with a business they can message. Fifty-six percent of consumers would rather message than call a business for customer service.[13]

And it works.

Studies reveal a 242 percent increase in open rates and a 619 percent increase in click rates on Facebook Messenger as opposed to email.[14] Although these will likely go down over time as people become more used to seeing messages from brands, for now it's a huge opportunity. As Facebook expert Molly Pittman says, "Messenger is an essential communication channel for businesses (and it's still experiencing rapid growth)."[15]

So, how can you use Facebook Messenger in your business? ManyChat is one of the tools that can help you set up a messenger bot or chatbot to better connect with followers. Think of it like creating an email newsletter list, but on Facebook. Advertising on Facebook Messenger is also important, and there are many new advertising products like Click-to-Messenger Ads, Sponsored Messages, and Messenger Home Placement.

Let's look at how this works in an example from one of my favorite companies.

For the 2017 Christmas season, Danish toy company LEGO decided to roll out its first messenger bot (named "Ralph") to better guide customers to find the best gift. It worked so well that they kept up the fun. In 2018, they started another campaign to directly compare the results on the messenger ads to the results of ads that simply served clicks to their website.

Their campaign started with some enticing video ads. One had a LEGO robot excited about a kid's great report card. "The perfect reward this term is a LEGO set!" Another had a LEGO robot standing in a field of Easter eggs that had LEGOs inside. "Give a really cracking LEGO present this Easter!" Both ads included the message that "Ralph the LEGO Chatbot is ready to help!"

A call to action button on the ad saying "send message" opened up into messenger and then the magic chatbot Ralph interacted with back-and-forth questions to the customer. The results of the A:B testing were clear when they compared the performance and efficacy of click-to-Messenger ads with click-to-website ads. The messenger ads won by a landslide, delivering a 71 percent lower cost per purchase.[16]

MAKE YOUR FACEBOOK FAN YOUR FRIEND (A IS FOR AUDIENCE)

At this point in your understanding of the SHARE model, you know how important it is to ensure that your Facebook marketing presence is about your follower and not your brand.

Now we need to go a step further and make sure that that follower is your friend. Use empathy to do so. Remember to cultivate it to increase engagement by doing one of three things: tell a great story, help someone, or ask questions.

When telling your story, be careful about too much content, especially in the form of curation from other sources. Although Facebook may not be the number one social media tool people use to get their news, 68 percent of users say it is a source of their news. That means curation is still super important. However, given the algorithm changes, you need to be much more selective with what you curate. Posting lots of content that doesn't receive engagement will tank the engagement of your entire page.[17] That's why a brand like Money Saving Mom, which posts many times a day with hot deals, has seen such an engagement drop-off and has resorted to creating a Facebook group. When the majority of your followers can't keep up with every single one of your posts, all of them will suffer.

When asking questions, or helping someone by answering one of *their* questions, make sure to follow up and like and respond to those interactions to further boost engagement.

EXPAND YOUR REACH (R IS FOR REACH)

When it comes to *reach* on Facebook, it's less about getting new followers than it is about engaging the ones you already have. Especially when we know that algorithms make it a challenge for users to see your content, it is essential to drive engagement with existing followers and fans to increase your chances of being seen by new folks.

First, make sure that your profile conveys your authority. Revisit chapter 5 for more tips on crafting a great profile that opens the story gap and prepares you to expand your reach.

Then, remember to think of ways to involve other people in your posts to get them seen by more people. Don't go overboard and tag everyone you know every time you post anything to get them to click. Do think of times when it makes sense for your brand to call out individuals.

Additionally, consider live video, which can increase interactions by as much as 600 percent.[18]

SUPERCHARGE YOUR FACEBOOK MARKETING WITH PAID TRAFFIC (*E* IS FOR EXCELLENCE)

There's a lot to be depressed about when you think of organic reach on Facebook. But when it comes to paid advertising, there's also a whole lot of good news. Studies show that brands who pay for advertising on social media are more than twice as likely to say social media marketing is "very effective" for their brand.[19]

This is especially true when it comes to Facebook. As the marketing firm HubSpot says, "Nowadays, Facebook is encouraging marketers to look at their fan bases as a way to make paid advertising more effective rather than using it as a free broadcast channel. Additionally, Facebook says you should assume organic reach will eventually arrive at zero. So, if you really want to reach your target audience on Facebook, you'll need to supplement your organic efforts with some paid advertising."[20]

Luckily, it works. Paid advertising on Facebook is a key way to fight the good fight to get your content in front of the consumers that you want to reach.

Kathryn Taylor used to head up marketing for All3Sports.com, a boutique store for triathletes in Atlanta. She and I first met at a StoryBrand Live Workshop, where she was working on figuring out who the character in her company's BrandScript really was. All3Sports.com had long dreamed of becoming the best triathlete store in the southeastern US, but Kathryn had seen there was a problem preventing them from reaching that goal. Their marketing was just too broad. As she says, "Talking to everyone is talking to no one." And they were talking to a whole lot of nobodies.

Her first challenge was to narrow down their character in the BrandScript. It was easier than she thought, and she soon determined that the ideal customer for All3Sports.com was a forty-five-to-fifty-five-year-old man living in the Atlanta area. That brought up other challenges, however. The nature of organic marketing on Facebook means that there is such a wide audience of potential consumers to tap into (2.2 billion, to be exact!), that local stores face a tougher time ensuring they aren't wasting their efforts speaking to people who aren't in their region. Luckily, Taylor found that paid Facebook advertising could address this problem directly and effectively.

With paid advertising, she could target a local audience, ensuring that her hard-earned marketing dollars were going only toward people who could realistically stop by the local store and then come back again and again. She saw such success with paid ads using this locally focused strategy that she began to wonder, "Is there such a thing as organic anymore?"

Although her question is a bit tongue in cheek, she does bring up a good point. When the possibility to enhance social media marketing with paid ads exists, why not pursue it?

Josh Cantrell, a Facebook ads specialist and StoryBrand Guide, tends to agree. He's also seen great success with Facebook ads for his clients, particularly by ensuring that all his advertising campaigns are closely aligned with the client's BrandScript.

Josh, who has also worked with clients in the triathlete space, told me about some of his StoryBranded video ads on Facebook that had done well. One ad, for a mobile app that triathletes can download to get triathlete-specific content and gear, said simply:[21]

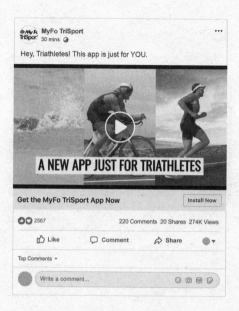

Its direct call to action encouraged application downloads.

Another cut right to the chase and encouraged the identity transformation that any hero seeks:[22]

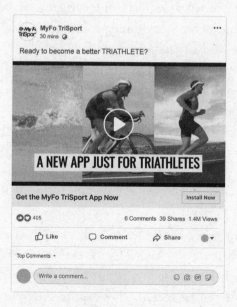

Another didn't even use words:[23]

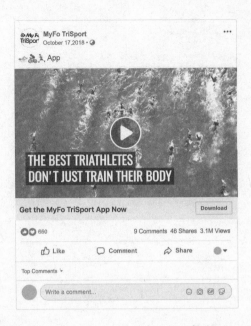

Now that's an ad that passes the StoryBrand grunt test. (The grunt test says that if I come to your website or see your ad and don't immediately understand that you sell shoes, cats, or triathlete gear, you don't pass.)

Other elements of the StoryBrand process are critical to remember in developing great paid ad campaigns on Facebook.

Pattern disruption is one of them. Just as the SB7 Framework encourages powerful hero images on websites, great images on paid advertising are also important.

Amy Porterfield runs an online marketing business that helps other online business owners build and sell products. Many of her ads understandably show her in her best light with high-quality professional photography.[24]

But not all.

And there's the big lesson. Pattern disruption is all about making people stop in their tracks. And sometimes that's with an unusual, eye-catching, or funny image.

See a few of the images in these quite *different* ads from Amy Porterfield.[25]

Amy Porterfield
Sponsored · 🌐

Would you like to grow your online business?

In this Inc interview, I share how to build an engaged, ready-to-buy audience online.

INC.COM
How I Went From Taking Notes for Tony Robbins to Building a 7 Figure Business

👍❤️ 405   6 Comments 39 Shares 1.4M Views

👍 Like   💬 Comment   ↗ Share   ●▼

Top Comments ▾

Write a comment...   😊 📷 🎬 🎁

Amy Porterfield
Sponsored · 🌐

When I did my first online course launch I set it live with an unfinished sales page 😮LOL!

And I ended up making only $267 in revenue after spending over $3000 creating it. 😩

Fast forward several years and many courses later, and i've developed a step by step system you can use to create your own online course that actually makes you a profit! ... See More

AMYPORTERFIELD.COM
[FREE TRAINING] Create a Profitable Online Course   Sign Up

👍❤️ 405   6 Comments 39 Shares 1.4M Views

👍 Like   💬 Comment   ↗ Share   ●▼

Top Comments ▾

Write a comment...   😊 📷 🎬 🎁

Amy Porterfield
Sponsored · 🌐

DON'T MISS OUT!

It's your last chance to enroll in List Builders Lab and claim all my incredible bonuses.

Click here right now to enroll >>>
http://www.amyporterfield.com/lblsp3b/

AMYPORTERFIELD.COM
[ENROLL NOW] List Builders Lab + Over $1500 Worth of Bonuses   Sign Up
Discover ALL the list building secrets I've learned on my journey to over 300K subscribers

👍❤️ 405   6 Comments 39 Shares 1.4M Views

👍 Like   💬 Comment   ↗ Share   ●▼

Top Comments ▾

Write a comment...   😊 📷 🎬 🎁

The length of the text in your ads can also make a difference.

Josh Cantrell has found that the short-form, action-oriented nature of ads works well for clients: "Long form content works for building awareness, but clicks to download are coming from shorter ads." (A click to download is an example of a direct call to action.) Additionally, one brand can find some long-form ads effective for certain products and some short-form ads effective for others.

As with anything, the success of a paid advertising campaign on Facebook is all about testing what works for you and your brand. Ultimately, Facebook can be an incredibly effective platform for social media marketing, and its ubiquity means that it's a sure bet for any brand. Using the SHARE model, wise businesses will see that building an engaged, organic basic and then jumping on paid advertising is where the real opportunity is.

CHAPTER 8

INSTAGRAM

In 2010, the founders of a location-based check-in platform called Burbn looked at the then-success of their biggest competitor, Foursquare, and saw the writing on the wall. In response, they decided to pivot their product to mobile photo sharing. It worked. Their new company, Instagram, was acquired by Facebook for nearly $1 billion two years later.[1]

With 1 billion users and 500 million daily users, Instagram has the highest engagement rates of any social media platform. Young people especially love it. A full 34 percent of millennials and 63 percent of teen internet users (adolescents between the ages of thirteen and seventeen) use it daily. Of all users, 22 percent log in at least once a day, and 38 percent check it multiple times a day.

Importantly for brands, users are shopping on the platform. Seventy-two percent say they have bought a product off Instagram. There are now 8 million business profiles on Instagram, and 43 percent of advertisers on Facebook also show their ads to Instagram followers.[2]

Given that Instagram users are the most engaged of any social network, your brand has a huge opportunity to open your story gap and start taking followers up your engagement ladder on this platform.[3] Furthermore, Instagram's restrictions on posting links directly into posts creates a forced constraint that reminds brands why the engagement ladder works in the first place.

Let's explore how your business can implement the SHARE model to reach social media success on Instagram.

ON CREATING AN ASPIRATIONAL STORY YOU WANT TO BE IN (S IS FOR STORY)

When you identify your character in your StoryBrand BrandScript, you also identify what your character wants on an external, internal, and philosophical level. The goal is to determine the exact transformation your character seeks so that you can market to this sense of potential. We call this an aspirational identity.

More than any other social media platform, Instagram excels at this. StoryBrand Guide Wes Gay, who no longer lives at his mother-in-law's, often refers his clients to the Instagram account of an American travel company, Away, for inspiration. Although they may be in the suitcase business, the vast majority of their posts don't have much to do with suitcases.[4]

Instead, they excel at invoking a sense of an aspirational identity and, as Wes says, "showing who you want to be with your suitcase in hand." Instead of TSA lines and overpriced fast food, the follower comes away thinking, *Put me in that story!*

Away's focus on aspirational identity and positioning the brand instead of pushing the product has been so successful that it led to a new business. In 2017, they launched (on Instagram) their new digital and print travel magazine focused on just such aspirational travel stories.

away Eat to live, live to eat. Explore the best of Tokyo with @mmcheng and @hannahjcheng, the sisters behind NYC's beloved @MimiChengs. 📷 @alyssainthecity #travelaway

1,478 likes

Photo courtesy of Alyssa Coscarelli (@alyssainthecity)

IS A PERFECT INSTAGRAM LIFE THE ENEMY OF A GOOD ONE?

Importantly, aspirational identity only works when you really know your character. After all, what inspires one person might turn off another.

Lisa-Jo Baker is a bestselling author who appeals to Christian moms who yearn to connect over how it *really* is. As she says, "Most days I can't find my car keys, my cell phone, or my mind. Most nights I think my heart will burst wide open from all the messy love stuffed inside it for those sweetly snoring kids. And many mornings I want to quit motherhood before I've even served the first bowl of Cheerios of the day."[5]

In her book *Surprised by Motherhood*, and on her popular Instagram account, she appeals to "women who are tired of hearing how things are supposed to be—perfect or simple or uncomplicated or easy—and passionate about hearing about how things *actually are*: hard, scary, stressful, wonderful, stretching, and still hard."[6] The hashtag she created, #surprisedbymotherhood, is now full of thousands of images from real moms everywhere, showing their "real, gritty, beautiful, everyday snapshots of motherhood."

Wes Gay says this is part of a new trend he calls "sloppy as spiritual." He believes the patron saint of the trend is Jen Hatmaker, the bestselling author who is a self-professed "lover of queso" and "mom to 5 maniacs."

Take a recent Thanksgiving Day post of Jen's. There was no set of polished silverware on a clean, white linen tablecloth. There was no perfectly posed picture of an impressively coiffed bunch. Instead, there were meat sweats.[7]

10,873 likes

jenhatmaker I didn't take any pics of our 25 member Thanksgiving feast today because I never have my phone out (🐢 fact). My sis took this selfie of us four sibs and our spoiled baby. What I should really post is a pic of my unbuttoned pants and meat sweats from my BIL's rotisserie turkey and prime rib, but that seems unkind to the Internet. I love these jokers. I love this day together. I love my Grandma King's carrot recipe which I have had at every Thanksgiving since 1974.

Her followers loved it.

---

lovelylia3

Same! Didn't take one single pic because I was really focusing on the people at the table and my sides versus documenting the moments 🙌

ritacoward

YES! . . . Jen, I Love that sweater! And . . . may I add . . . these eyes!!! 🖤 Life carries us away, but we must stay close to those most dear. 😊

Wes says this idea that "the dishes are dirty and the house is a mess, but I've got Jesus and a cup of grace" has become a clear trend in the Christian digital marketing space. It is a guiding light for what might be a larger shift in how to think about aspirational identity on social media.

Lysa TerKeurst is another powerful voice in the Christian women's world. Her latest book, *It's Not Supposed to Be This Way*, chronicles an incredibly challenging time in her own life and encourages women to keep going even when things don't go as planned. When she was then invited on a TV show to promote her book, things *definitely* didn't go as planned.[8]

Instead of sweeping the interview under the rug, she highlighted it to her many followers. It made them feel connected to her as a real person, sharing what it means to fall down, pick yourself up, and laugh along the way.

At the end of the day, the way you approach being authentic on social media when it comes to aspirational identity is all about knowing your character. Authors Lisa-Jo Baker, Jen Hatmaker, and Lysa TerKeurst appeal to Christian women seeking to live their best lives amid the chaos

of the everyday. Away appeals to everyday travelers who want a more peaceful and upgraded travel experience.

Away does curate great images, notes Wes, but they don't do so in a way that makes you feel burdened that you're not a global traveler. Instead, they aim to turn the impossible into the accessible. As Wes says, when he looks at an Instagram post of a suitcase rolling through a café in France, he knows he might not be doing that anytime soon, but he also knows it isn't so impossible anymore. He has the tools. Or rather, the suitcase.

It also reminds us that, on social media, the image is no longer the story itself but rather the launching point. In figuring out what matters most to the brand—the story—and removing the heavily curated filters, brands can get back to what's most important.

Take MailChimp, an email marketing company that prides itself on its quirks and on bringing together people who don't fit in. On Instagram they do an excellent job of using laugh-out-loud images to pull people into their brand story.[9]

In their case, the image doesn't represent the story but serves as a funny, eye-catching launching pad to tell it.

HOW TO POST ON INSTAGRAM
(*H* IS FOR HOW)

When it comes to your social media budget, Instagram requires that users not only think about the message they want to post but the format they want to post it in. Here are the types of posts you can create:

A Classic Post: The classic Instagram post is the mainstay of your Instagram profile. It is an image with text.

A Video Post: Video posts are videos you upload that are between two and sixty seconds long.

Instagram Live: Just like on Facebook, on Instagram you can do live video.

An Instagram Story: When IG came out with the Instagram Story, folks cried the death of Snapchat. And for good reason. A story on Instagram is similar to a video on Snapchat. It disappears after twenty-four hours.

CURATION

Quality curation is always a key way to make deposits into your social media bank account. On Instagram curation is a bit different than on other platforms. Although there are third-party tools you can use to repost others' content, the reality is that most of the time you create your own. That said, to ensure that you are making enough deposits into your social media bank account, there are some creative ways to curate that allow you to merge other people's content with your own.

Pyne & Smith Clothiers, an ethically made fashion company in California, is a brand that does this well. In this post, the brand introduces an external concept—wabi-sabi—as a way to open up a discussion that is likely in line with the interests of their followers.[10]

The responses showed that it resonated:

> **@mayres**
> I love the concept. My kids have perfectionist tendencies (as do I) and get frustrated by mistakes so I taught them about wabi sabi and now they make "wabi sabi art" where there are no rules and no mistakes. They are always my favorite.

Importantly, to open the story gap the clothier made the decision to include an image of one of their products. The result? Some commenters started to do the "selling" for them, recognizing the product they purchased and gushing over it:

> My current favourite dress 👗 been on repeat all fall 🍁 and going strong into winter ❄️ no regrets whatsoever about investing in this dress!

ON INSTAGRAM, THE HERO IS YOUR FOLLOWER (*A* IS FOR AUDIENCE)

Cali'flour Foods is a company that makes low-carb, grain-free cauliflower pizza crusts. They've seen great success with StoryBrand. In the first year after taking their company through the process, they increased their annual gross profit by a multiple of twenty-four.[11] Social media is one of their greatest marketing tools.

Given their location in Northern California, when the devastating 2018 fires hit their area, they knew it was more important than ever to focus on what mattered most to their 115,000 followers (many of whom were local) during the difficult time.[12]

califlourfoods ...

In light of recent events in our beautiful county, we will be pushing our grand opening to a later date.

CALI CONCEPT KITCHEN

653 likes

califlourfoods We recently announced that we would be hosting a grand opening for our first brick & mortar, Cali'Concept Kitchen. However, in light of recent events in our beautiful county, we will be pushing our grand opening to a later date. Now is the time to focus our efforts towards doing everything we can to help our community during this tragic time 🙏

-
Cali'Concept Kitchen will still be open Tuesday, & you're more than welcome to still stop by, but our celebration will be at a later date in the coming months. We'll be sure to let you know once details are confirmed 🖤

-
#prayforparadise #prayforcalifornia #buttecounty #chico #paradisefire #californiastrong #chicostrong

califlourfoods ...

350 likes

califlourfoods Dearest Cali'flour Family,

Thank you for your outpouring of love for our friends and families affected by the fires. Your thoughtful messages are heard and deeply appreciated by each of us. A quick update to ease worried minds: our team is safe, and our home office will be serving as a collection site for donations and supplies. The farms where we grow our cauliflower and our production facility are also far beyond the reach of the fires. As such, we are grateful to be able to continue normal operations and deliver you fresh, quality products without delay.

This blessing will be paid forward to take care of our neighboring businesses and community members who were not so lucky. Now through midnight on Tuesday 11/13, 50% of every sale will go towards purchasing emergency supplies for the victims of the fire. Thank you in advance for your support in this effort!

In lieu of Cali'Concept Kitchen's grand opening on Tuesday, our team will be visiting local evacuation centers to hand out pizzas, personal hygiene products, clothing, and blankets.

Thank you again for your continued prayers and compassionate action for those who have lost everything. In our darkest hours, this community inspires more hope in me than ever before.

In togetherness,
Amy Lacey & The Cali'flour Team

MOVING UP THE ENGAGEMENT LADDER

The goal of the engagement ladder is to get your follower to move closer to closing the story gap and responding to your call to action. That might mean becoming more engaged on Instagram, clicking over to your website, signing up for your email newsletter, or buying your product or service.

Let's look at a few ways brands do this well on Instagram.

TAGGING

Tagging people on Instagram works to encourage others to respond and create engagement. Recently I endorsed the new book of Allison Fallon, the writer mentioned in the introduction, who had hired a marketing firm that didn't understand the difference between direct marketing and brand marketing. Since my endorsement appeared on the cover of *Indestructible*, when people started posting it to Instagram they often tagged me in the post. This allowed me to see the post and then chime in once again with how much I loved the book.

DIRECT MESSAGING

Due to the restrictions on links on Instagram and the increasing issues with the Facebook algorithm not showing Instagram posts to followers unless they are engaged, direct messages (DMs) have become more important. One tactic is for a brand to purposely create ways to encourage your potential customer to engage in a DM with the brand.

My college pal Ramit Sethi, CEO of I Will Teach You to Be Rich, did this recently when he posted a picture about his recent trip to a luxury resort in India.[13]

In the post, he encourages folks who are interested in participating in a luxury Indian vacation he is organizing to DM him.

ramit   ...

2,135 likes

ramit Years ago, I told my brother-in-law that I'd been wanting to stay at @theoberoiudaivilas, an absolutely amazing hotel in India. But I told him, "Once you stay there, where do you go next? I don't want to go there too soon." He told me something I'll never forget. "Ramit, if you can afford to go and you're healthy enough, you should go. There'll always be other hotels, but you never know what will happen tomorrow." Call it the Hotel Metaphor for Life: If you can do it today, do it. You never know what will happen tomorrow.

We stayed here on the Udaipur portion of our honeymoon. It's now my favorite hotel in the world. The luxury, the staff, the food, and the memories we created here...I will never forget it. And we will be back!

By the way, if you've been following along on my honeymoon stories and you're interested in taking a luxury trip to India with me next year, send me a DM.

ENCOURAGING OFFLINE ENGAGEMENT

South Shore Grill Hawaii serves great Mexican food in Honolulu. One offline fan wrote them a postcard thanking them for their grub.[14]

They posted it on Instagram, showing a great testimonial, and also reminding their followers to take their love for South Shore Grill *offline*.

And then there's this.

When Berkeley-based clothing store Cotton Basics had a phone line glitch, they posted a handwritten note about how to contact them.[15]

AMALIA'S THREE-STEP INSTAGRAM GROWTH STRATEGY (*R* IS FOR REACH)

Long before Amalia McGibbon began working at Facebook, she had built up a large following on her hobby photography Instagram account, @amaliastudios. Since she's my BFF, I asked her what she did to get so many followers. Here is Amalia's Simple Three-Step Instagram Growth Strategy:

1. Take great pictures.
2. Use lots of relevant hashtags.
3. Repeat.

Years later, this is still the secret sauce.

Axe and the Oak is a craft distillery that makes award-winning whiskey. They used StoryBrand to clarify their marketing. On Instagram they offer an effective combination of lots of great photos and lots of hashtags to boost their reach.[16]

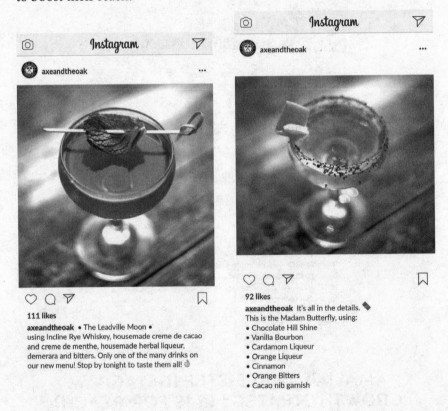

My own husband can also attest to how well a combination of great images with great hashtags can work. Jose is an architect and vintage guitar nerd who restores and sells vintage guitars. In 2018, he started a new account, @ponchoguitars, following Amalia's strategy and quickly built up a large following of folks interested in the niche topic.

FIGURE OUT WHAT WORKS FOR YOUR FOLLOWERS (*E* IS FOR EXCELLENCE)

As with all platforms, understanding what works for *your* followers is the most important thing. My husband's niche guitar account learned this lesson well.

When Jose's vintage guitar posts started to get shared more widely and his account began to grow, he realized the importance of testing different kinds of images. Using Amalia's formula—great pictures, lots of hashtags, repeat—he began to dig into what pictures really worked.

What he found was pretty weird. As a photographer, he has an eye for what's a good photo and what isn't. He found that posting objectively good photos worked. No surprise there.[17]

But what worked even better? When he posted the same photo, but from a less aesthetically pleasing angle. (Shot from above.)

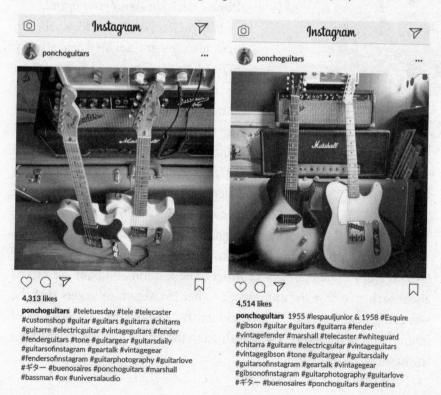

4,313 likes

ponchoguitars #teletuesday #tele #telecaster #customshop #guitar #guitars #guitarra #chitarra #guitarre #electricguitar #vintageguitars #fender #fenderguitars #tone #guitargear #guitarsdaily #guitarsofinstagram #geartalk #vintagegear #fendersofinstagram #guitarphotography #guitarlove #ギター #buenosaires #ponchoguitars #marshall #bassman #ox #universalaudio

4,514 likes

ponchoguitars 1955 #lespauljunior & 1958 #Esquire #gibson #guitar #guitars #guitarra #fender #vintagefender #marshall #telecaster #whiteguard #chitarra #guitarre #electricguitar #vintageguitars #vintagegibson #tone #guitargear #guitarsdaily #guitarsofinstagram #geartalk #vintagegear #gibsonofinstagram #guitarphotography #guitarlove #ギター #buenosaires #ponchoguitars #argentina

He would tell you that there is no question that the front-facing image of the same guitar is a better image. Would his followers agree? Not a chance.

He also learned to play around with timing, figuring out what worked for his followers.

Ultimately, it doesn't matter that Jose thinks the images look weird or that he personally prefers to scroll Instagram at night rather than at lunchtime. It's about what the other vintage guitar nerds on his account want.

As Jen Hatmaker reminds us, on Instagram as in all your marketing efforts, you are never the star. Your follower is.[18]

But even though your customer is the hero, you are their guide. And the guide is important. That's why you do make the ultimate decision about your brand.

When Carolyn Rivers Mitchell, the circus manager at Club Med, had already amassed seventy thousand followers on her Instagram account, she decided she wanted to stop curating circus content and start building her own personal brand as a performer. When she changed her Instagram name and started posting different types of content, she did lose seven thousand followers. But in the end, she had her brand back.

Instagram

jenhatmaker

STAR
DRESSING
ROOM
209

7,443 likes

jenhatmaker Backstage at the #moxiematterstour in OKC, and this dressing room really gets me. 😣

You have never met two people with less "star power" than me and @nicholenordeman. The day I start acting a fool who thinks the dressing room needs to flatter her, y'all take me out and take me out hard. Of course, a real prima donna wouldn't be wearing the exact same outfit she wore to speak last weekend which was well documented on social media, but I already told you I wear the same five outfits so don't act surprised.

Similarly, missionary blogger Joy Forney is a fan of ethically made fashion from Pyne & Smith Clothiers, the fashion company we talked about earlier. When she announced to her Instagram followers that she was going wear the same dress every day for a whole year, she got a lot of interest and new followers who wanted to follow the experience through the hashtag #onedressoneyear.

And then she took it back.[19]

Your brand is the guide, and as the guide it is your job to tell your audience what you can and can't help them with.

joyforney

902 likes

joyforney Hello again everyone. I've had a nice little break from this space. I'd like to let you know that if you are here because of my #onedressoneyear challenge, you can go ahead and unfollow me now. With the help of my therapist, my darling husband, and some beloved friends, I have come to realize that I've been really hard on myself since my husband's accident in October.
So in an effort to be kinder to myself I am letting go of some limits I had placed on myself, the dress challenge being one of them.
Gentle is the word for me this year, and I hope to share more of this journey as I follow my Gentle Shepherd who has been so kind and faithful. He offers so much grace in our times of trial. He is so good.
Thank you for being here with me! I truly treasure each one of you and think of my little space on insta as a sacred space to learn and grow together as we lean into Christ.
Much love, Joy
I'll be back here on the regular with gentle encouragement, for you and me, in the areas of godliness, #tenitemwardrobe, mothering, and living simply. 🖤 If you have no idea what I'm talking about, you can find out more about my husbands accident if you look for the square with a white flight shirt with tire marks on it. 🖤 #titus2woman #godisgood #heisfaithful

CHAPTER 9

TWITTER

In 2006, Twitter launched as the result of a two-week side project incubated by some of the employees at Blogger.com. In the original vision, it was a microblogging platform that could send short, real-time updates.

At the time, the folks at Blogger.com had found and promoted my blog about traveling around the world, living in an orphanage in Kenya, and running a small nonprofit. When they launched Twitter, they recommended I start tweeting. When I did, they put up a blog post on the Twitter.com blog. (It's still there, although I had a different username at the time.) For a while, my account was featured on the homepage.

Very quickly, a whole bunch of way more interesting people joined the platform. Ashton Kutcher loved it, and its use by Obama during the 2008 presidential elections was a big turning point. Right around that time Twitter's cofounder, Biz Stone, came to England where I was in business school. The day I met him was the day that the BBC was trying to interview him because there was a report that Facebook wanted to buy Twitter for $100 million. (Twitter said no.) Over drinks, Biz and I talked about the importance of using Twitter proactively as a tool for social innovation and impact, and he offered me an internship. I went and stayed for five years.

Twitter, like many social media platforms these days, has faced enormous criticism in recent years. I get it. I do. I also believe that it can still be used well by brands of all sizes to make a difference in the world.

Let's look at how you can best implement the SHARE model on Twitter.

YOUR STORY ON TWITTER IS BIGGER THAN YOUR BRANDSCRIPT (S IS FOR STORY)

Remember, the premise of the social media bank account is that roughly 80 percent of the time you make deposits in the form of valuable content and roughly 20 percent of the time you make withdrawals when you close the story gap and call a customer to action.

On Twitter, the nature of the short, real-time updates makes it easier than other platforms to consume, reshare, and create content. As a result, many brands fall into the trap of swaying too far from their BrandScript too much of the time. That's why it's important to remember these two truths when opening your story gap and keeping followers active on your engagement ladder:

Your BrandScript is a guide.

Your BrandScript is *just* a guide.

Patagonia is a brand that does a great job of handling this tension. On Twitter, they don't send their followers pictures of fleece jackets all day. Neither do they retweet pictures of wet cats.

Instead, they double down on their wider mission to "build the best product, cause no unnecessary harm, use business to inspire and implement solutions to the environmental crisis." Specifically, they set themselves apart as a Twitter account that provides valuable information about the environmental crisis as well as content about great gear. At the end of the day, if you are interested in the environment, they are a great account to follow. This means that even if I don't need a new jacket this year, I will stay on the engagement ladder. By continuing to consume their content, you can bet that when I do need one, I'll make a purchase from them.

Here are some examples of the content they post to Twitter:[1]

@patagonia

New report proves that three-quarters of rivers in the Balkans are crucial life support systems for the entire ecosystem and should be totally off limits for hydropower: http://pat.ag/pbd24 #savetheblueheart

 @patagonia

In a report released on #BlackFriday, take 10% off the size of the U.S. economy by 2100 from damage related to climate change. @nytimes

 @patagonia

Love the outdoors? Here are 8 Senate races where we can make the difference.
@hatchflymag: http://pat.ag/r4zge

Holidays, national events, or times of crisis are other obvious moments where it makes sense to stray a bit from your BrandScript to address what's going on in the real world.

Sustainable fashion brand Everlane was one of a number of brands in the US to close their doors on election day.[2]

 @Everlane

Sorry, not sorry. We're off to vote today. If you can, you should too! 🇺🇸 Find your polling place here: https://www.vote.org/polling-place-locator/ …P.S. Our retail stores will be opening later today so our team can get out and vote. Today's hours: 1pm - 8pm

The tweet did a good job of informing the public, providing some practical information about their store hours, and also sticking to their brand ethos and personality.

CURATION ON TWITTER (*H* IS FOR HOW)

More than any other social media platform, Twitter is where people go for news. That's why the art of curating information on Twitter is so essential for brands to fully understand.

When the large nonprofit organization World Vision worked on a campaign to end gender-based violence, they remembered to use curated content in their social media budget. One day, the World Vision Twitter account tweeted a link to a BBC article showing that new UN data estimates that 137 women are killed every day around the world as a result of gender-based violence. Then they added their own note as well:[3]

 @WorldVision

It's not okay that 1 in 3 women experience physical or sexual violence in their lifetime. During the next two weeks we're sharing how your support is helping us address gender-based violence to change the lives of women and girls. #EndGBV #16Days #OrangeTheWorld

This strategy allowed them to send valuable information to their followers on two fronts: the new statistics in the BBC article and the new campaign World Vision was running. Ultimately, this tied their campaign into the curated content.

QUESTIONS CAN MAKE IT ABOUT YOUR AUDIENCE (*A* IS FOR AUDIENCE)

The *A* in the SHARE model is all about your audience. Asking questions and helping others (often by answering questions) are two of the key ways to make it about your followers. Since Twitter excels at both of these functions, it's no wonder that journalists rely on it so much. Following the 2018 death of missionary John Allen Chau on a remote island in the

Indian Ocean, a number of media outlets wrote in-depth articles about problems in the missionary field. When the *New York Times* reached out to *Failed Missionary* author Corey Pigg, he posted the query to his followers to help crowdsource some stories.[4]

 @failmissionary

I just got off the phone with The New York Times and we are helping them with on an article. They are investigating the role of the missionary and they want to hear from YOU. They want to know why you got into missions, why you got out and what you're up to today.

He got a number of responses and retweets from followers eager to help him (and help the journalist) to source the story:[5]

 @aslipperyslope2

Just submitted my story!

 @theKevinGarcia

CALLING ALL FORMER MISSIONARIES! The New York Times wants former missionary perspectives, and I KNOW WEVE GOT THEM. click the link, fill out a quick form. simple as that.

Another way to make it about your audience is to regularly retweet when people write about you. As a nonprofit organization, World Vision regularly retweets donors who tweet about them. This helps to not only thank a donor but to encourage others to make donations as well.[6]

 @RnBaking

Got an early Christmas gift - probably the best I have had for a long time. #proudchildsponsor @WorldVisionPH @ WorldVision

Cali'flour Foods also did this to convey a positive testimony for their product and increase their authority.[7]

 @Califlourfoods

It's the best! ----> It's what's for dinner. 2 days ago I made lasagna using @califlourfoods pizza crusts in the place of noodles. It was a huge hit. Delicious and filling 🖤 🖤 Served it tonight with a side…

HASHTAGS AND INFLUENCERS THAT GO FAR (*R* IS FOR REACH)

Hashtags are a critical part of using Twitter. We went deep into how to use them in chapter 5. For now, remember the two rules to make a great hashtag:

1. Be as general as you can get away with.
2. Don't use a hashtag that most people already associate with something else.

TWITTER WAS MADE FOR INFLUENCER OUTREACH

Over the years, some of the best stories about brands using Twitter to grow have related to the ways they have connected with influencers and built beneficial, supportive, long-term relationships. That's because Twitter is a social media platform that allows you to technically write a message to anyone you want—they don't have to be a friend or connection. And people do. My favorite example of this comes from Global Citizen Year, which I shared in chapter 5.

As a reminder, here's how to reach out effectively to an influencer on Twitter:

Find the niche. First things first, start following the key people and hashtags in your niche. Most importantly, narrow it down to go after people who may be a "reach" for your brand but are not an impossibility. If you run a nonprofit serving adoptive parents, go for an engaged blogger in the adoption space, not Oprah.

Find the influencers. Start following the key individuals in these niches. Stay organized with your outreach by not going after too many people at once. On Twitter, for example, you can create a private list of target influencers. This allows you to remember to check in a few times a week by responding, retweeting, or mentioning someone you want to pursue.

Start engaging. Now start engaging with those influencers to try building a conversation that has nothing to do with your "ask." Remember what we discussed in chapter 5? You may find that one of the best ways to start talking *to* someone is to first talk *about* someone. Often influencers know who their number one fans are, especially if those individuals offer valuable content of their own.

WHAT TO DO WHEN HATERS WILL HATE (*E* IS FOR EXCELLENCE)

Kirsten Powers is one of CNN's most popular political analysts because she tells it exactly like it is. On TV, she excels in equal measure at intelligent commentary and withering side eye. Because it's politics, sometimes the on-air debates can get ugly.

On Twitter, it's *always* a bloodbath. As a woman, she gets an extraordinary amount of hate messages about her physical appearance. (Her hair, which is incidentally gorgeous, is a favorite topic.) Every day Kirsten gets tweets that my publisher would never reprint here.

Sometimes she ignores them.

Sometimes she fights back with positivity by getting peers and other influencers to highlight respectful, balanced articles from both sides of the fence with the idea that the good will rise to the top.

A HYPE GROUP

Last year, Kirsten Powers created a private group on Twitter with some friends. It worked like this: when people found or created great content that needed a boost to get going, we nudged each other to share. In the social media world, this is called a "hype group," and it can work on a variety of platforms.

And sometimes Kirsten retweets the terrible things that are said in order to help others, a practice that Chelsea Clinton also engages in on Twitter. By shedding a light on the reality of online bullying, we can take steps to one day change it.

CHAPTER 10

LINKEDIN

As an older social media network, one of LinkedIn's greatest strengths is its ability to stay (relatively) focused on its original mission of creating the world's largest professional network. LinkedIn boasts more than 500 million registered users in more than two hundred countries, with 100 million actively using the platform each month. A full 80 percent of LinkedIn members reportedly consider professional networking to be imperative to their careers, and executives from all Fortune 500 companies are members.

In recent years, LinkedIn has shifted more and more into content creation. More than one hundred thousand articles are posted each week, and the purchase of online course platform Lynda.com has solidified LinkedIn's commitment to content. This is critical for brands to understand, as LinkedIn now offers an important avenue for social media marketing beyond its primary purpose in networking and recruiting.[1]

ON LINKEDIN, PEOPLE TELL YOUR BRAND'S STORY (*S* IS FOR STORY)

Of the top four social media platforms, LinkedIn users are the most engaged after Instagram.[2] Since LinkedIn relies on written content much more than Instagram does, I would argue that it is the social media platform that most depends on great written content.

So how does a brand tell a great story on LinkedIn?

Through people.

The key is that the creation of long-form content still depends on individuals. That's why LinkedIn influencers—who are top content producers with tons of followers—are people, not brands. So what can a brand do?

First, short-form content such as status updates, which appear in your main news feed, is something that brands can share. This means that curation is an important way to help you deliver value and make a deposit into your social media bank account. Given the high engagement rates, ensure that you stick to quality content so that you train your followers to click on and read your posts. This way they will be just as likely to click when you make a withdrawal to close the story gap and move someone up your engagement ladder.

IBM does a great job of curating useful short-form content and posting it to their timeline on their Facebook page.[3] For example, here they share an article one of their own SVPs David Kenny wrote for VentureBeat.[4]

IBM

The cognitive era needs what we at IBM call "thoughtful pioneers."

"Why we need pioneers in cognitive computing"

When it comes to long-form content, though, things are different. Since blog post content on the LinkedIn Pulse platform comes from individual profiles, you need real people in your business to write it.

The CEO of Lemonade, an insurance company that uses machine learning and AI to better serve their customers, did a great job doing just that. Although the company account has a robust twenty-three thousand followers, the CEO has almost as many, and the chief insurance officer also has a respectable four thousand. That's because the Lemonade executives are the ones who publish the long-form articles on LinkedIn Pulse. The Lemonade business profile then points to the content in the news feed.

Arguably the most successful campaign they ran was called "The Transparency Chronicles," in which they shared behind-the-scenes stories from their business. The stories were not always positive, and that's what brought in the readers.[5] "This kind of content can really stand out and gain traction in feeds full of corporate messaging, especially when contrasted against many competitors in the insurance industry."[6]

HOW TO CRAFT GREAT CONTENT ON LINKEDIN (*H* IS FOR HOW)

So how can you start creating great content on LinkedIn?

Create a personal profile. This is the bread and butter of LinkedIn, and the number one priority for your time. As your favorite flight safety videos explain, put on your own oxygen mask first before assisting others. That's because unlike on other social networks, your LinkedIn personal profile is essential to helping promote your business. First create yours, then create your business's.

Create a business profile. This is the profile for your business that you will set up. You'll want to ensure that all of your stakeholders and employees have connected their personal profiles to your business one.

Create a group. Setting up a LinkedIn group around a topic or a special interest is a great way to encourage engagement.

Create blog posts. As explained above, on LinkedIn the personal profiles create the long-form content through blog posts. This is a great chance for one or more of your brand's employees to start writing content or syndicating what you already post somewhere else for maximum reach. Remember to craft a footer on every blog post that uses language from your BrandScript, like your one-liner, to link back to your brand's website.

KNOW YOUR CHARACTER TO KNOW WHEN TO POST

As with all social media platforms, it's important to know your character when you think about the best time of day and day

---

of the week to post. Since LinkedIn is a professional platform, it makes sense that one study showed that the best times to post are between Tuesday and Thursday, either early in the morning, at lunch, or early in the evening after work.[7] Depending on the business your brand is in, this will affect when you want to schedule your content.

IT'S NOT ABOUT YOU (A IS FOR AUDIENCE)

As a LinkedIn influencer, I have nearly half a million followers and more than ten thousand connections on LinkedIn. I have spent time crafting a great profile. All that to say, I thought I knew what I was doing. It turns out, I was making it too much about me. Thankfully, Marshall Goldsmith turned that all around.

Marshall Goldsmith is known as America's #1 Executive Coach, and he has been the trusted coach to luminaries such as Alan Mulally, former CEO of Ford Motors, and Jim Yong Kim, former president of the World Bank. Goldsmith is also a bestselling author who has sold millions of business books. In the past few years, he started a scholarship program called the MG100 to give back everything he's learned to one hundred thought leaders. When I was named a member of the MG100, I learned that I didn't just have a lot to learn in terms of leadership. I also had a heck of a lot to learn about LinkedIn.

LinkedIn is a place to show authority, but more than that it's a place to show that you care about your audience. And Marshall does. When he decided to launch the application process for the MG100, his announcement about the endeavor ended up being the most viewed post on LinkedIn that year. It garnered more than seventeen thousand applications to his program. The reason was anything but intentional.

As Marshall explains, the main point of the post was to put a link to the application where people could apply. A link he promptly forgot.

Understandably, he soon started to receive tons of comments saying more or less the same thing: "Where's the link, Marshall?"

And that's when he did something smart.

Instead of just updating the main blog post with the link, his team responded to *every single comment* asking for it. And, as Marshall says, "the LinkedIn wheel started churning!" Every time they responded to a comment, it gave the post a further bump, ultimately helping it become the most viewed post on LinkedIn that year.

When it comes to the "LinkedIn wheel," as Marshall calls it, Julian D'Souza also had a very good experience. His had to do with a hamburger. One day the Stones Corner Hotel manager took to LinkedIn to post a picture of a very large hamburger—and to ask his followers what they should name it. Responses were through the roof.

Julian D'Souza
Director, The World Food Markets & Events
Layered with fillings like pulled pork, bacon, mac 'n' cheese and chorizo crumbs, you won't be short on inspiration to name our newest burger beast. Put your bun puns to the test and name our burger with the lot - the winner scores two tickets to the Australia vs India showdown at the Gabba, January 15th

---

In three weeks, the post got 8,000 comments and generated 25,000 likes. And, similar to Marshall's experience, Julian saw that comments seeded comments. Every time one of those 25,000 people liked the post, it showed up in their connections' timelines as well.[8]

Lemonade, the insurance company, had a similar experience when it came to their highly engaged posts. As their head of communications and content, Yael Wissner-Levy, said, "We were surprised by the good karma that we were getting from people—who thought insurance would be such a social media-worthy subject—and that kind of led us to engage with them even more so. We aim to answer everyone that writes to us on LinkedIn, and love to watch and participate in the conversations that develop around us."[9]

The lesson?

Do anything to get your audience to engage with your post, and then do anything to engage with them.

And use images when you can. "According to data LinkedIn has shared, images have a 98 percent higher comment rate and links can double engagement."[10]

If you don't have an image of a large hamburger on hand, a good video will do. LinkedIn reports that videos can increase share rate by 75 percent.[11]

One final way to boost engagement is to ensure that you tag relevant parties in your posts. These days, every time Marshall posts he makes sure to tag relevant people in the MG100 to help boost the post. As with CNN's Kirsten Powers, a "hype group" is a small community that can help to share each other's content. Closed groups do this frequently for the public posts of their members. (This same idea works well on Facebook too.)

EXPAND YOUR REACH WITH A KILLER PROFILE (*R* IS FOR REACH)

Since your business card on LinkedIn is your profile, making sure it effectively conveys your authority is essential.

First up is a great image. LinkedIn profiles with photos get twenty-one times more profile views. Additionally, adding a profile picture makes you fourteen times more likely to be found on LinkedIn and thirty-six times more likely to receive a message.[12]

My friend and celebrity photographer Jeremy Cowart explained at the LinkedIn Success Summit what it takes to have a great LinkedIn profile photo. The big key? Make it the real you.

"You know when you see a photo of yourself if it feels natural or not." As Jeremy says, you know if you're really smiling or fake smiling. Go for the real smile. In his own profile, he's not even looking directly at the camera, but that doesn't matter because his real-life laugh more than makes up for that. "I wasn't even trying to take a headshot," he says of his current profile picture. "Somebody was literally making me laugh."[13] Jeremy also suggests going for a photo that is relatively up to date. Your LinkedIn profile photo, like your online dating one, shouldn't feature the you of 1999.

For the background header, Jeremy recommends a natural landscape with nice color tones. Although some people go for a logo or a styled tagline in that section, it can be very busy for the average follower and take away from the main thing: your profile. Think of it like creating too many calls to action.

The same applies for the background of a business profile. For the main image, however, you'll want a great logo as opposed to an individual's image.

On a personal profile, you'll also want to list your skills and have endorsements for those abilities. There are fifty thousand skills currently listed on LinkedIn, and you want to be associated with as many as you reliably can, and then seek endorsements for them. Why? Because it increases your page views. It turns out that listing more than five skills will get you up to seventeen times more profile views.[14]

Also, make sure to use LinkedIn's recommendations feature. You can directly solicit recommendations from people, or you can wait until they flow into your inbox. Whatever you do, please read your pending recommendations before adding them to your profile. Some time ago, I received a "recommendation" from someone I had never heard of that read: "Claire lacks accountability and has no responsibility that should be outside of waiting tables at Denny's. I've spent weeks nearly a month trying to get her to understand that she has to be accountable and she is noncompliant. Even with technology she claims to easily understand and comprehend cannot answer simple emails."

Although I had never heard of that person in my life, they claimed to be "senior" to me but had never directly managed me. Huh? Needless to say, I am quite glad this "recommendation" for another Claire was not automatically added to my LinkedIn profile and that I got the chance to reject it!

Whitney Johnson is the bestselling author of *Build an A-Team* and the founder of the consulting firm WLJ Advisors.[15] Since she has almost

2 million followers on LinkedIn, she knew when she took her company through the StoryBrand process that it was just as essential to implement the BrandScript into her LinkedIn presence as it was into her website.

The first thing she did was ensure that her profile conveyed her BrandScript messaging: be the leader everybody wants to work with. Then she began looking at the content she produced.

It's important for every business to do what Whitney did. Analyze your status updates and blog posts to ensure that they truly open the story gap and connect with your overall BrandScript.

TRYING NEW THINGS (*E* IS FOR EXCELLENCE)

Finally, remember that going off script works.

On its most basic level, your LinkedIn personal profile is for work connections and your Facebook personal profile is for personal ones. That's why, historically, people don't post much personal content on LinkedIn.

Marshall Goldsmith's 1.2 million followers know him on LinkedIn for his work, not his family life.

That's why he was so surprised with the response he got to a personal Thanksgiving Day post of a photo of his family celebrating the holidays. Although the post wasn't reshared extensively in leadership circles as a piece of curated content, it garnered incredible engagement in the form of hundreds of comments. Part of this is the nature of pattern disruption in storytelling. Marshall posts more regularly about leadership advice and is thus known in the world for this work.

This also goes to show the power of both empathy and pattern disruption in storytelling. Although the Thanksgiving post didn't further promote Marshall's BrandScript as an executive coach, it did further promote him as a human celebrating an important day off of work with his family. And that's why it was so effective. Followers used to his business advice loved the chance to engage on a more intimate and conversational level.

Although LinkedIn is still the professional network it was when it launched nearly twenty years ago, its expansion into content creation and dissemination offers a way to build stronger connections with your professional network. Ultimately, this gives businesses the chance to share their StoryBrand more often to sell more.

CHAPTER 11

COMPLEMENTARY PLATFORMS

Pinterest, Reddit, Quora, and YouTube

Last year I went to Pinterest in San Francisco to learn about the philosophy behind the platform. As cofounders Evan Sharp and Ben Silbermann explained, Pinterest is about creating a life you love. Evan said, "Words are the language of knowledge; images are the language of dreams." This means that Pinterest is more about curating your dream life for yourself than making your life *look* great for others.

So how can brands benefit from this behavior?

Erica Chan Coffman runs a huge online lifestyle blog, *Honestly WTF*, that curates fashion, art, travel, interior design, and DIY content. Pinterest is perfect for her readers, and her 6 million followers love nothing more than a stylish image of an adorably designed nursery, a clean pink desk, a fashionable rattan purse, or a stacked gold necklace. Many times they save the images she curates, click through, and buy. (Erica often gets a small commission.)[1]

If your brand doesn't specialize in beautiful images of beautiful things, should you forget about Pinterest?

Not necessarily. Ruth Soukup first built a huge Pinterest following around her popular blog, *Living Well Spending Less*. Pinterest is full of moms interested in recipes and DIY crafting solutions, so even though

Ruth's posts weren't necessarily ready for the pages of *Martha Stewart Living* like Erica's, they still attracted a large following.[2]

Her efforts also showed that businesses that aren't design focused can also have success. When Ruth started a new business, Elite Blogging Academy, she proved just that. On that account she doesn't share images, but rather eye-catching graphics that link to informative articles about blogging. (And, sometimes, information about how to enroll in her Academy.)[3]

More than 2.5 million people a month now consume her blogging-related content.

Ultimately, even though Pinterest is less about sharing with others than about curating for yourself, it can still be a great tool for some brands.

REDDIT AND QUORA

Earlier in the book we talked about why asking questions is such a good strategy to generate engagement on social media. In fact, question-asking is so effective that there are entire platforms built up around it, and Instagram now has an Ask Me Anything function you can use in their Stories.

In-depth questions or ones that beg different opinions can be even more effective. This is the entire basis of the social media platform Quora, which gets 300 million monthly unique users. With more than four hundred thousand topic question threads, it's clear that people love sharing what they know.[4]

Reddit's AMA platform works according to the same idea. AMA stands for "Ask Me Anything" and refers to a written online interview that occurs between a host and the public participants who attend the written interview and ask questions. Currently, there are 18 million users on Reddit, and the most famous AMA ever hosted was in 2012 when Barack Obama attracted 3 million page views. On Reddit you can start a chat about anything, and folks will respond with questions.[5]

As I write this, a teacher in Borneo and a small rodent are both offering to answer questions about their different areas of expertise.[6]

I'm coming to the end of 3 years teaching in the Brunei jungle, Borneo AMA

I'm 27, my partner and I have had great time here and travelled to some awesome places near and far to here!

My rat's hands work on my phone screen, I'm gonna let her answer some questions. AMA. Her name is Peach and she's 1 year old. She's hairless. She's extremely pink.

What more could I want?

To make Reddit work for your brand, follow these two key guiding principles:

1. Bring in someone people want to ask questions of.
2. Create context around the open-ended discussion.

Everyone wants to ask questions of a rat. And of Bill Gates. Luckily for us, they both offer opportunities. Bill Gates, in fact, does annual AMAs on Reddit, and he does a good job of coming with context around the discussions.[7]

He introduced one by saying:

> I'm back for my third AMA. I'm happy to talk about anything. Philanthropy, technology, what it's like to drink water made from human waste.... (Short answer: Just like drinking any other kind of water, except that people get a little freaked out by the whole idea.) I hope you'll take a few minutes to look at the annual letter that melons and I just published (gatesletter.com). This year we make a case that in the next 15 years, life will improve faster for people in poor countries than it ever has before.[8]

And remember, even if you're not using Reddit, the strategy of a one-off or serial AMA works on other platforms.

YOUTUBE

YouTube can be a great tool for many brands. One of the simplest ways to get started is by including video testimonials in your social media marketing.

Earlier we talked about Hard Exercise Works, the high-intensity fitness center in Florida with dozens of locations. They came to me concerned that their marketing was directed too much toward elite athletes and not enough toward the real people who work out in their gym. In their BrandScript, we identified that their character was an everyday person and the internal problem she faced was not believing she could do the hard work to get in shape.

That's why it was so important that the testimonials they used in their marketing visually show that real people could really do hard workouts. And that's where YouTube came in.

Remember that video testimonial they had showing women in their gym reacting to a *New York Times* article that said that women couldn't do pull-ups? Few things could be more motivating to women sitting at home, not sure they can do it.

That said, the biggest mistake people make when it comes to social media marketing on YouTube is not realizing that many of the same strategies that apply to written content also apply to video. The key is in remembering that even on other platforms your content is often a mix of different types of media.

Remember the #LetThemLeave campaign, which successfully freed three missionaries? That campaign kicked off with a YouTube video where Thomas Kemper, general secretary of the United Methodist Church, encouraged folks to sign the petition and share it using the hashtag on Twitter, Facebook, and Instagram.

Crossover like this happens all the time. On Reddit, a celebrity who does an AMA proves it is really them by including an image or video at the start of the AMA. Bill Gates likes to take it to the next level. In one of his annual AMAs, he recorded a funny YouTube video to go along with the written content in a Reddit AMA to prove it was him.[9,10] Another time, he sent a package of gifts to a Reddit user who participated in his AMA. One of the virtual items in the package was a video from famed YouTube vlogger Hank Green.[11] It was a great way to continue the social media conversation and engagement across multiple platforms.

Speaking of Hank Green, he and his brother John Green may just be the kings of YouTube vlogging. Back in 2007, they began a fun project where they stopped communicating via text or emails for an entire year and instead conversed only through daily public vlogs posted on YouTube. The success of their still-thriving "vlogbrothers" YouTube channel has now expanded into eleven other channels and more than 12 million subscribers.[12]

Although the Green brothers do use other forms of social media these days, their bread and butter is YouTube. One reason is that YouTube offers a way for users to accessibly watch and rewatch videos in a way that other social media platforms haven't completely mastered (which means that content creators can reliably earn from advertising dollars).

Green describes his bizarre career, "I'm just interested in stuff and so like I will find myself on Wikipedia just reading about things and part of the reason is that's part of my job. . . . finding out interesting things about the world turns into an episode, and that episode turns into money. So it's kind of work, which is wonderful."[13]

Thankfully for the rest of us, it delivers great value. Teachers regularly praise the Green brothers for entertaining, educational content that works well in the classroom.

Importantly, the Green brothers show that success with video marketing on YouTube isn't about saying the exact right words, but rather adhering to the overall message. Or rather, creating multimedia content that shares your BrandScript.[14] In their case: "creating resources that allow for more valuable interaction in the classroom."[15]

Sometimes your stories on YouTube don't need any words at all. As a parent of three toddlers in the digital age, I am constantly amazed by the riveting content that exists on YouTube for humans who can't even speak yet.

Take toy unboxing videos. Or mixing slime. Or a recent favorite: lava.

Whatever form of media you use—text, images, video—your brand's social media marketing goal is the same: to share a clear, engaging story. And if an eleven-minute video of a lava flow working tirelessly to slowly crush a Coke can isn't a clear, engaging story, I just don't know what is.

AFTERWORD

If you've read this far, then I bet I know something about your business. Every day your brand works hard to ensure that potential customers find out about your product or service and then stick around to become raving fans. And you know that social media is one of the most important, ubiquitous, and cost-effective marketing methods available to you to amplify your message.

The problem is that social media is notoriously confusing and ineffective. From deciding which platform to use to figuring out what content to post, it's hard to know what to do, and it's easy to waste a whole bunch of time and money trying to figure it out. Even if your brand has already implemented the SB7 Framework in your marketing, you know that applying your BrandScript to a social media platform is by no means a straightforward process. Until now, there hasn't been a simple StoryBrand solution to ensure your social media has the clear messaging you need to move the needle.

That's where the SHARE model for social media success comes in.

This framework helps brands like you to understand what matters when it comes to effective social media marking and exactly how to implement that in your business. It works for those who are new to the StoryBrand process and who are old hats at StoryBrand.

In this book we've explored how the model works and how to use it on the most important social media platforms. My hope is that you'll take what you've learned and implement it today to finally see social media success for your brand.

ACKNOWLEDGMENTS

My thanks are many. Here are a few.

To Don Miller—a decade ago in the woods of Canada, you said we should collaborate on something and now we did. The honor is mine.

To the whole StoryBrand team—including Betsy, Tim, JJ, Koula, Melissa, Avery, and Alex, in memory. You are building a company that is changing the face of marketing, and it has been a joy to cheer from the sidelines.

To the smart publishing people—Wes Yoder of Ambassador Literary, and Sara Kendrick and Amanda Bauch of HarperCollins. For sharp minds and sharper pens.

To the many individuals, startups, and brands who provided the case studies for this book and for the larger development of the SHARE model for social media success. Ever since my days at Twitter, I have relied on others' willingness to pull back the curtain on their own digital media use to understand what works and what doesn't in the wild. Thank you.

And finally, to the dedicated fire marshal of my home, Jose, and our resident arsonists, Lucia, Santi, and Mateo. I need more toes to stay on the tips of.

In the words of my children, who I hope will never learn that it is actually not the appropriate thing to say when a book comes to an end, amen!

THE SHARE MODEL

As you now know, SHARE stands for *story*, *how*, *audience*, *reach*, and *excellence*. Here is a convenient overview of the model, which was also presented in chapter 1.

STORY

Use your StoryBrand BrandScript on social media to open the story gap, move your followers up an engagement ladder, and close the story gap when you call them to take action.

Remember:

- The first step in the SHARE model is *story*. Content is queen, and the content for your social media marketing comes from your StoryBrand BrandScript.
- Social media marketing is usually *brand marketing*, not *direct marketing*. That means that most of the time your goal is not an immediate sale.
- Effective social media marketing should always *open the story gap*, move followers up an *engagement ladder*, and then *close the story gap* with a *call to action*.

- Your *social media bank account* only thrives with give-and-take. Remember the 80/20 rule. Deposit value 80 percent of the time by opening the story gap with your content. Then, 20 percent of the time make a withdrawal by closing the story gap with a call to action.
- To balance your *social media budget*, vary the types of content you deposit and withdraw. Content should come from different content envelopes, including things like curated content, original content, articles, quotations, statistics, testimonials, direct calls to action, transitional calls to action, impactful images, selfies, video, etc.

HOW

Learn the practical logistics of *how* to post your content.

Remember:

- Take the *Social Media Brand Evaluation* to determine your brand's priority social media platforms (see appendix 2). Concentrate on the platforms that matter most to your brand.
- To decide how many accounts you need on each platform, remember that the fewer accounts you have, the better.
- Who posts matters less than you think. When to post matters more. Time of day, day of the week, and season of the year are all considerations.
- Third-party tools can help with scheduling, curating, and analytics. Hootsuite, Buffer, Sprout Social, and Sendible are all good platforms that offer different benefits.
- Consistency is important. Ensure that you create a *social media schedule* and *social media editorial calendar* that work for your audience and your brand's bandwidth.
- Use pattern disruption and selective break-taking to your advantage.

AUDIENCE

Your social media marketing should be about your *audience*, not your brand.

Remember:

- Your brand is not your hero; your customer is.
- Your customer (or potential customer) is your follower. Reframe your social media account to make it about them.
- Cultivating empathy on social media matters to building a relationship with your customers and reaching long-term success. Remember this equation: Empathy + Connection = Social Media Engagement.
- Generate empathy (and engagement) by telling a great story, helping someone, and asking questions.
- Don't post and ghost. Great social media marketing requires real-time connection and engagement with your audience.

REACH

To amplify your brand on social media, it's important to expand your *reach*.

Remember:

- Craft a killer social media profile that increases your authority and opens the story gap by using your BrandScript.
- Prioritize your existing social media tribe over new followers every day of the week.
- The three ways to get new followers on social media are to create great content, use influencer marketing, or pay for advertising to boost either of those strategies.
- Great hashtags can put great content on steroids. When crafting

a hashtag, be as general as you can without using a term people already associate with something else.
- Concentrate on reaching influencers in a way they like. Remember that it's a long-tail game that relies on finding the right niche, finding the right influencer, and engaging with them over time.

EXCELLENCE

Fine-tune your social media marketing efforts to reach long-term *excellence*.

Remember:

- Always ask yourself how you can get followers to want in on your story.
- The real-time nature of social media means that you don't always know what's going to happen. Make that a good thing.
- On social media, it's about rolling with the punches. If your brand makes a social media mistake, own up to it. Fast.
- Social media gives your customers a public place to share their grievances. Sometimes they will do just that. If the comments aren't offensive, let the dialogue take place, and don't delete the negative content. Whenever you can, try to turn a negative conversation into a positive one.

SOCIAL MEDIA BRAND EVALUATION

This evaluation will help your business determine which social media platforms will work best for you. Once you take it, you will know which platform is your top priority, and where you should spend most of your marketing efforts.

Please answer the following questions on behalf of your brand:

1. How many followers do you have on each of the following platforms?
   ○ Twitter _____
   ○ Facebook _____
   ○ LinkedIn _____
   ○ Instagram _____
   ○ Pinterest / Reddit / Quora / YouTube / Other _____
2. How many people are you following on each of the following platforms?
   ○ Twitter _____
   ○ Facebook _____
   ○ LinkedIn _____
   ○ Instagram _____
   ○ Pinterest / Reddit / Quora / YouTube / Other _____

3. Subtract the number of people you follow from the people following you on each platform and write out that number:
   ○ Twitter _____
   ○ Facebook _____
   ○ LinkedIn _____
   ○ Instagram _____
   ○ Pinterest / Reddit / Quora / YouTube / Other _____
4. Which platform has the highest number? _____
5. Which platform has the second-highest number? _____
6. What platform do you *think* most resonates with your audience? (Don't overthink this; go with your gut.) Another way to ask this question is: Where do you think your audience spends their time on social media?
   ○ Twitter _____
   ○ Facebook _____
   ○ LinkedIn _____
   ○ Instagram _____
   ○ Pinterest / Reddit / Quora / YouTube / Other _____
7. On which platform do you have the most engagement? (Although deep analysis isn't required, we do want a real sense here.)
   ○ Twitter _____
   ○ Facebook _____
   ○ LinkedIn _____
   ○ Instagram _____
   ○ Pinterest / Reddit / Quora / YouTube / Other _____
8. Which platforms do your competitors use most?
   ○ Twitter _____
   ○ Facebook _____
   ○ LinkedIn _____
   ○ Instagram _____
   ○ Pinterest / Reddit / Quora / YouTube / Other _____
9. Which platform do you or your social media manager or marketing team have a personal affinity for?

○ Twitter _____
○ Facebook _____
○ LinkedIn _____
○ Instagram _____
○ Pinterest / Reddit / Quora / YouTube / Other _____

10. Which platform(s) do you already know how to use and/or does the individual or team managing your social media already know how to use?
○ Twitter _____
○ Facebook _____
○ LinkedIn _____
○ Instagram _____
○ Pinterest / Reddit / Quora / YouTube / Other _____

Get Your Results: Write out the number of times you responded with each platform in questions 4–10:
○ Twitter _____
○ Facebook _____
○ LinkedIn _____
○ Instagram _____
○ Pinterest / Reddit / Quora / YouTube / Other _____

The platform with the highest number is your priority platform. The second highest number is your secondary platform, and so on in that order.

Your Priority Platform is: _____

Your Secondary Platforms in the following order are: _____

> If you learn better by video, access a free five-video minicourse at SocialMediaMadeSimple.com.

STORYBRAND RESOURCES

THE STORYBRAND "SOCIAL MEDIA MADE SIMPLE" ONLINE COURSE

If you learn best in video and want to dive even deeper into the social media framework, this online course walks you through the process described in this book, to ensure that you are applying the SB7 Framework well in your social media marketing. Get the course at SocialMediaMadeSimple.com.

THE STORYBRAND MESSAGING COURSE

If you would like to take the complete SB7 course on your own time and at your own pace, the StoryBrand Messaging Course walks you through the creation of your BrandScript, while giving plenty of examples and inspirational success stories. Once you're done with the course, you will have a message you can use to create websites, keynotes, elevator pitches, and much more. Get the course at storybrand.com/online.

THE STORYBRAND LIVE MARKETING WORKSHOP

If you want to spend dedicated time clarifying your message, while surrounded by exciting peers who are also working to grow their companies, sign up for our live workshop. Our facilitators will show you endless examples of successful messaging and coach you, to make sure you're creating the perfect BrandScript for your company. Not only this, but we will review best practices in simple marketing techniques that will give you a plan moving forward. Get away for two days, and walk away with the entire process finished and ready for execution. Our live workshops will get you results. Register today at storybrand.com.

THE STORYBRAND PRIVATE WORKSHOP

Walking your people through the StoryBrand Framework in the comfort of your own office is the next step to aligning your team, growing your business, reducing marketing costs, and creating a common language that excites and inspires your team. You'll spend two days clarifying your StoryBrand BrandScript and unifying your team, and our facilitators will even take a look at your existing marketing materials once your BrandScript is created. The private workshop process takes one and a half days, and your company will never be the same. Get more information at storybrand.com/privateworkshops.

BECOME A CERTIFIED STORYBRAND GUIDE

If you'd like to give great marketing advice by helping people clarify their message and execute the StoryBrand Marketing Roadmap, apply to become a StoryBrand Certified Guide. StoryBrand Certified Guides are approved through an interview process and then listed in our online directory. Those who have a knack for marketing and messaging and want to start a coaching business, along with existing coaches looking to increase their value, are welcome to apply. Corporations wanting to certify members of their team may also apply. You can learn more at storybrand.com/guide.

BECOME A STORYBRAND CERTIFIED AGENCY

If you have a design agency and want to use the SB7 Framework to create marketing collateral for your clients, you can be listed in our Agency Certification database by taking our agency certification program. Each program is custom comprised for each agency, based on how many designers, copywriters, and project managers your team includes. Find out more at storybrand.com/agency.

NOTES

INTRODUCTION: WHAT EVERYONE GETS WRONG ABOUT SOCIAL MEDIA

1. Claire Diaz-Ortiz (@claire), Twitter, April 5, 2004, 1:31 a.m., https://twitter.com/Claire/status/452362820760633344.

2. Jacob Shelton, "The Worst Viral Marketing Campaigns," Ranker, accessed April 15, 2019, https://www.ranker.com/list/viral-marketing-fails/jacob-shelton.

3. Dan Tynan, "The 10 Worst Viral Marketing Campaigns," CIO, August 12, 2008, https://www.cio.com/article/2434318/the-10-worst-viral-marketing-campaigns.

4. See information about becoming a StoryBrand Guide or a StoryBrand Certified Agency in the StoryBrand Resources section in appendix 3.

5. Pushpay (@pushpay), Twitter, July 14, 2016, 11:00 a.m., https://twitter.com/Pushpay/status/753650421663617024.

6. Wes Gay (@wesgay), Twitter, October 3, 2016, 6:10 p.m., https://twitter.com/wesgay/status/783112010074615808.

7. Alejandro Reyes (@alejandroreyes), Twitter, October 3, 2016, 7:55 p.m., https://twitter.com/alejandroreyes/status/783138441894572036.

8. Jason Falls, "Understanding the Direct Vs. Brand Marketing Conflict," Social Media Explorer, September 30, 2013, https://socialmediaexplorer.com/content-sections/tools-and-tips/direct-vs-brand-marketing/.

9. Falls, "Understanding the Direct Vs. Brand Marketing Conflict."

10. "The Honest Company," Wikipedia, updated April 1, 2019, https://en.wikipedia.org/wiki/The_Honest_Company.

11. Shannon Barbour, "Rob Kardashian was Forced to Sell His Failing Sock Line to Momager Kris Jenner," *Cosmopolitan*, November 14, 2018, https://www.cosmopolitan.com/entertainment/a25105076/kris-jenner-rob-kardashians-sock-line/.

CHAPTER 2: *STORY*: TELLING A GREAT SOCIAL MEDIA STORY

1. Donald Miller, *Building a StoryBrand: Clarify Your Message So Customers Will Listen* (Nashville: HarperCollins Leadership, 2017), 20.
2. Miller, 37.
3. Miller, 22.
4. Miller, 38.
5. Margaret Rouse, "What is the Pareto Principle?" WhatIs.com, updated August 2013, https://whatis.techtarget.com/definition/Pareto-principle.
6. In honor of financial guru Dave Ramsey's budgeting envelope system, we're calling each content category in your social media budget a content envelope. To see more on Dave Ramsey's envelope system for budgeting your finances, go to DaveRamsey.com.
7. Resharing is a secondary tactic because on many platforms it is not given the same algorithmic prominence.
8. Miller, *Building a StoryBrand*, 201.

CHAPTER 3: *HOW*: WHO'S THE KING OF YOUR SOCIAL MEDIA ACCOUNT?

1. Victoria Chang, "Obama and the Power of Social Media and Technology," *The European Business Review* (May–June 2010), 16–21, https://people.stanford.edu/jaaker/sites/default/files/tebrmay-june-obama.pdf.
2. Chang, "Obama and the Power of Social Media."
3. Russell Goldman, "Obama Promises a New Dawn of American Leadership," ABCNews.com, November 5, 2008, https://abcnews.go.com/Politics/Vote2008/obama-promises-dawn-american-leadership/story?id=6182036.
4. Chang, "Obama and the Power of Social Media."
5. "Barack Obama on Social Media," Wikipedia, updated January 20, 2019, https://en.wikipedia.org/wiki/Barack_Obama_on_social_media.
6. Nancy Scola, "Obama's Very First Tweet, and Other Haiti Relief Social Media Wins," Tech President, January 18, 2010, http://techpresident.com/blog-entry/obamas-very-first-tweet-and-other-haiti-relief-social-media-wins; American Red Cross (@redcross), Twitter, January 18, 2010, 11:38 a.m., https://twitter.com/RedCross/status/7915529685.
7. "Barack Obama on Social Media," Wikipedia; Hashtags (@hashtags), Twitter, June 30, 2011, 8:34 a.m., https://twitter.com/hashtags/status/86457611662262272.

8. Colin Campbell, "Barack Obama and Bill Clinton Just Had a Cheeky Twitter Exchange," *Business Insider*, May 18, 2015, https://www .businessinsider.com/barack-obama-and-bill-clinton-had-a-twitter -exchange-2015-5; Bill Clinton (@BillClinton), Twitter, May 18, 2015, 12:57 p.m., https://twitter.com/POTUS44/status/600407380279566336.

9. Tsh Oxenreider (@tshoxenreider), Instagram, https://www.instagram.com /tshoxenreider/.

10. Tsh Oxenreider (@thesimpleshow), Instagram, April 30, 2008, https://www .instagram.com/p/BiMxuTJAsah/.

11. Claire Pelletreau, ClairePells.com.

12. Pritha Bose, "6 Hootsuite Alternatives You Must Try," Sprout24, April 9, 2019, https://sprout24.com/4-hootsuite-alternative-you-must-try/.

13. Sendible, https://www.sendible.com/.

14. Rani Molla and Kurt Wagner, "People Spend Almost as Much Time on Instagram as They Do on Facebook," Recode, July 25, 2018, https://www .recode.net/2018/6/25/17501224/instagram-facebook-snapchat-time -spent-growth-data.

15. Jen Hatmaker (@jenhatmaker), Twitter, August 10, 2006, 7:40 p.m., https://twitter.com/jenhatmaker/status/763565644763828225; Kristin Henry (@krby0404), Twitter, August 11, 2006, 7:06 a.m., https://twitter .com/Krby0404/status/763738256949116928; Jen Puckett (@jen4redemption), Twitter, August 10, 2006, 7:45 p.m., https://twitter.com/jen4redemption /status/763567091714633728.

16. Claire Diaz-Ortiz (@clairediazortiz), Instagram, December 11, 2016, https://www.instagram.com/p/BN40muXBPzG/.

CHAPTER 4: *AUDIENCE*: SOCIAL MEDIA—IT'S NOT ABOUT YOU

1. Webster (1979), quoted in P. J. Manney, "Empathy in the Time of Technology: How Storytelling Is the Key to Empathy," *Journal of Evolution and Technology* 19, no. 1 (September 2008): 51–61, https://jetpress.org/v19 /manney.htm.

2. Manney, "Empathy in the Time of Technology."

3. Brené Brown, *Dare to Lead: Brave Work, Tough Conversations, Whole Hearts* (New York: Random House, 2018), 163.

4. Suren Ramasubbu, "Expecting Empathy on the Internet," Huffington Post, updated July 7, 2016, https://www.huffpost.com/entry/expecting-empathy -on-the-internet_b_7737962; P. J. Manney, "Is Technology Destroying

Empathy?" Live Science, June 30, 2015, https://www.livescience.com/51392
-will-tech-bring-humanity-together-or-tear-it-apart.html.

5. Manney, "Empathy in the Time of Technology."

6. Ramasubbu, "Expecting Empathy on the Internet."

7. Franklin M. Collins, "The Relationship Between Social Media and
Empathy" (master's thesis, Georgia Southern University, 2014), 37, https://
digitalcommons.georgiasouthern.edu/cgi/viewcontent.cgi?article
=2189&context=etd.

8. Miller, *Building a StoryBrand*, 48 (see chap. 2, n. 1).

9. Tara Parker Pope, "Why Women Can't Do Pull-Ups," *New York Times*,
October 25, 2012, https://well.blogs.nytimes.com/2012/10/25/why
-women-cant-do-pull-ups/.

10. Claire Diaz-Ortiz (@claire), Twitter, April 11, 2018, 2:30 p.m., https://
twitter.com/Claire/status/984181973068500992.

11. Jenna Worthen (@jennaworthen), Twitter, April 11, 2018, 6:42 p.m.,
https://twitter.com/JennaWorthen/status/984245240231006208;
Tsh Oxenreider (@tsh), Twitter, April 11, 2018, 5:27 p.m., https://twitter
.com/tsh/status/984226470548697089; Tsh Oxenreider (@tsh),
Twitter, April 11, 2018, 6:17 p.m., https://twitter.com/tsh/status
/984239067754790912; Nish Weiseth (@nishweiseth), Twitter, April 11,
2018, 2:33 p.m., https://twitter.com/NishWeiseth/status
/984182712876482560.

12. Leilah Janah (@leilahjanah), Instagram, November 25, 2018, https://www
.instagram.com/p/Bqmtk2AB40-/.

13. Scott Williams (@scottwilliams), Twitter, March 23, 2008, 5:52 p.m.,
https://twitter.com/ScottWilliams/status/447717465091768320.

14. CT / Caroline (@fox_trot35), Twitter, October 5, 2018, 8:09 a.m.,
https://twitter.com/fox_trot35/status/1048228614372773890; Southwest
Airlines (@SouthwestAir), Twitter, October 5, 2018, 8:12 a.m.,
https://twitter.com/SouthwestAir/status/1048229565624025088; Mike
Anderson (@VUmander), Twitter, November 4, 2018, 11:14 a.m.,
https://twitter.com/VUmander/status/1059162014147379200; Southwest
Airlines (@SouthwestAir), Twitter, November 4, 2018, 11:20 a.m.,
https://twitter.com/SouthwestAir/status/1059163441544318977.

15. Molly St. Louis, "Here's How Brands Should be Using Facebook Live,"
Adweek, January 3, 2018, https://www.adweek.com/digital/heres-how
-brands-should-be-using-facebook-live/; Funny or Die, "The Great Pulp

Debate: Pulp, No Pulp, or Some Pulp?," Facebook, October 24, 2016, https://www.facebook.com/funnyordie/videos/10154616395923851/.

16. Jess Gaertner (@jess.holdthespace), Instagram, October 17, 2018, https://www.instagram.com/p/BpDpIFVAJPu/.

17. Balanced Bites (@balancedbitespodcast), Instagram, October 12, 2018, https://www.instagram.com/p/Bo2opRSFTfu/.

CHAPTER 5: *REACH*: INCREASE YOUR REACH TO AMPLIFY YOUR BRAND

1. Jack Dorsey (@jack), Twitter page, accessed May 7, 2019, https://twitter.com/jack.

2. Mark Zuckerberg (@zuck), Facebook page, accessed May 7, 2019, https://www.facebook.com/zuck.

3. Donald Miller (@donaldmiller), Twitter page, accessed July 28, 2019, https://twitter.com/donaldmiller.

4. StoryBrand (@StoryBrandWorkshops), Facebook page, accessed May 7, 2019, https://www.facebook.com/StoryBrandWorkshops/.

5. Amy O'Leary, "Christian Leaders Are Powerhouses on Twitter," *New York Times*, June 2, 2012, https://www.nytimes.com/2012/06/02/technology/christian-leaders-are-powerhouses-on-twitter.html.

6. Carolyn Rivers Mitchell (@flyingcarolina), Instagram, March 12, 2019, https://www.instagram.com/p/Bu7Czb4AnLB/.

7. Wikipedia, s.v. "Chris Messina (open-source advocate)," last modified July 26, 2019, 19:28, https://en.wikipedia.org/wiki/Chris_Messina_(open-source_advocate).

8. Chris Messina (@chrismessina), Twitter, August 23, 2007, 2:25 p.m., https://twitter.com/chrismessina/status/223115412.

9. Linda Bloom, "Church Seeks Release of Jailed Missionary," United Methodist Insight, June 26, 2018, http://um-insight.net/in-the-world/advocating-justice/church-seeks-release-of-jailed-missionary/.

10. United Methodist Church (@unitedmethodistchurch), Instagram, June 26, 2018, https://www.instagram.com/p/BkfcDHWnPCW/?hl=en&taken-by=unitedmethodistchurch.

11. Global Ministries, The United Methodist Church (@umcmission), Twitter, June 30, 2018, 2:02 p.m., https://twitter.com/umcmission/status/1013165897480056832.

12. Global Ministries, The United Methodist Church (@umcmission), Twitter,

June 28, 2018, 12:00 p.m., https://twitter.com/umcmission/status /1012410309166936064.

13. Thomas Kemper (@kemper_t), Twitter, July 1, 2018, 3:32 a.m., https://twitter.com/kemper_t/status/1013369741233143808.

14. Linda Bloom, "Last of Detained Missionaries Arrives Home," United Methodist Insight, July 16, 2018, https://um-insight.net/in -the-church/umc-global-nature/last-of-detained-missionaries-arrives -home/.

15. Global Ministries, The United Methodist Church (@umcmission), Twitter, July 27, 2018, 5:00 a.m., https://twitter.com/umcmission/status /1022813856836476928.

16. General Board of Global Ministries, Facebook, September 3, 2018, https://www.facebook.com/GlobalMinistries/videos/818796888329103/.

17. Tanya Sichynsky, "The 10 Most Influential Hashtags in Honor of Twitter's Birthday," *Chicago Tribune*, March 21, 2016, https://www.chicagotribune .com/bluesky/technology/ct-twitter-hashtags-10-most-influential-20160321 -story.html.

18. Sichynsky, "The 10 Most Influential Hashtags."

19. Alyssa Milano (@Alyssa_Milano), Twitter, October 15, 2017, 1:21 p.m., https://twitter.com/alyssa_milano/status/919659438700670976?lang=en.

20. Paulina Cachero, "19 Million #MeToo Tweets Later: Alyssa Milano and Tarana Burke Reflect on the Year After #MeToo," Makers, October 15, 2018, https://www.makers.com/blog/alyssa-milano-and-tarana-burke -reflect-on-year-after-me-too.

21. The Global Citizen Year case study originally appeared in Claire Diaz-Ortiz, *Twitter for Good: Change the World One Tweet at a Time* (San Francisco: Jossey-Bass, 2011), 56.

22. Global Citizen Year (@GlobalCitizenYr), Twitter, May 20, 2009, 4:26 p.m., https://twitter.com/GlobalCitizenYr/status/1864880251.

23. Global Citizen Year (@GlobalCitizenYr), Twitter, September 18, 2009, 10:02 a.m., https://twitter.com/GlobalCitizenYr/status/4082946438.

24. Global Citizen Year (@GlobalCitizenYr), Twitter, October 29, 2009, 1:32 p.m., https://twitter.com/GlobalCitizenYr/status/5268416432.

25. Global Citizen Year (@GlobalCitizenYr), Twitter, January 11, 2010, 1:02 p.m., https://twitter.com/GlobalCitizenYr/status/7642792877.

26. Global Citizen Year (@GlobalCitizenYr), Twitter, December 16, 2009, 9:17 a.m., https://twitter.com/GlobalCitizenYr/status/6736042083.

27. Global Citizen Year (@GlobalCitizenYr), Twitter, March 11, 2010, 9:59 a.m., https://twitter.com/GlobalCitizenYr/status/10332879620.

28. Global Citizen Year (@GlobalCitizenYr), Twitter, March 23, 2010, 1:29 p.m., https://twitter.com/GlobalCitizenYr/status/10942387178.

29. Nicholas Kristof (@NickKristof), Twitter, March 24, 2010, 3:36 a.m., https://twitter.com/NickKristof/status/10973051527.

30. Global Citizen Year (@GlobalCitizenYr), Twitter, March 24, 2010, 7:52 a.m., https://twitter.com/GlobalCitizenYr/status/10982610964.

31. Global Citizen Year (@GlobalCitizenYr), Twitter, July 30, 2010, 7:49 a.m., https://twitter.com/GlobalCitizenYr/status/19914803675.

32. Nicholas Kristof (@NickKristof), Twitter, October 19, 2010, 11:43 a.m., https://twitter.com/NickKristof/status/27858608812.

33. Global Citizen Year (@GlobalCitizenYr), Twitter, October 19, 2010, 12:30 p.m., https://twitter.com/GlobalCitizenYr/status/27861834112.

34. Global Citizen Year (@GlobalCitizenYr), Twitter, November 5, 2010, 4:36 p.m., https://twitter.com/GlobalCitizenYr/status/692867492225024.

35. Claire Diaz-Ortiz, *Twitter for Good: Change the World One Tweet at a Time* (San Francisco: Jossey-Bass, 2011), 126, 127.

36. Brené Brown (@brenebrown), Instagram, September 15, 2018, https://www.instagram.com/p/BnxXomWniIF/?taken-by=brenebrown.

37. Jen Hatmaker (@jenhatmaker), Instagram, September 15, 2018, https://www.instagram.com/p/BnxfAwvhNCd/?taken-by=jenhatmaker.

CHAPTER 6: *EXCELLENCE*: EXCELLING AT SOCIAL MEDIA MARKETING

1. American Red Cross (@RedCross), Hootsuite, February 15, 2011, 11:24 p.m. (tweet deleted).

2. Gloria Huang (@riaglo), Twitter, February 16, 2011, 4:40 a.m., https://twitter.com/riaglo/status/37853906642014208.

3. American Red Cross (@RedCross), Twitter, February 15, 2011, 9:40 p.m., https://twitter.com/redcross/status/37748007671832576.

4. Dogfish Head Brewery (@dogfishbeer), Twitter, February 16, 2011, 6:19 a.m., https://twitter.com/dogfishbeer/status/37878672522215424.

5. McDonald's (@McDonaldsCorp), Twitter, March 16, 2017, 1:16 p.m. (tweet deleted).

6. Elena Cresci, "McDonald's Tweets Go Rogue with 'Tiny Hands' Jibe at Donald Trump," *Guardian*, March 16, 2017, https://www.theguardian.com

/us-news/2017/mar/16/disgusting-excuse-president-mcdonalds-tweets
-trump-tiny-hands.

7. Chrysler Autos (@ChryslerAutos), Twitter, March 9, 2011 (tweet deleted).

8. Tim Nudd, "Chrysler Throws Down an F-Bomb on Twitter," AdWeek, March 9, 2011, https://www.adweek.com/creativity/chrysler-throws -down-f-bomb-twitter-126967/.

9. Anthony Noto (@anthonynoto), Twitter, November 24, 2014 (tweet deleted).

10. Frank Danna, "I Survived the Unicorn Frappuccino," Medium, April 20, 2017, https://blog.markgrowth.com/i-survived-the-unicorn-frappuccino -c9840894960.

11. Mary Bowerman, "Starbucks Barista Loses It Over Unicorn Frappuccino Mania," USA Today, April 20, 2017, https://www.usatoday.com/story /news/nation-now/2017/04/20/starbucks-barista-loses-over-unicorn -frappuccino-mania/100686874/.

12. Natalie Koltun, "Mobile Campaign of the Year: Starbucks Unicorn Frappuccino," December 4, 2017, https://www.mobilemarketer.com/news /mobile-campaign-of-the-year-starbucks-unicorn-frappuccino/510799/.

13. Koltun, "Mobile Campaign of the Year."

14. Koltun, "Mobile Campaign of the Year."

15. Regulus (@kamikayzee), "#unicornfrappuccino What it looks like vs what it tastes like," Twitter, April 19, 2017, 7:28 p.m., https://twitter.com/KamiKayzee /status/854884459807555584; Little Bby Breakfast (@cauldron_farts), "my friend just sent me a pic of the unicorn frappuccino and it looks like a cupful of soap from various public restrooms," Twitter, April 18, 2017, 4:41 p.m., https://twitter.com/cauldron_farts/status/854473247345315840; Jon Acuff (@jonacuff), "Just got my kids unicorn frappuccinos for our 10pm delayed flight to Disney that now lands at 1AM," Instagram, April 21, 2017, https://www.instagram.com/p/BTK2Q1rhoK4/.

16. "Facebook Gone Wrong: 5 Fails Brands Can Learn From," Business 2 Community, May 21, 2014, https://www.business2community.com /facebook/facebook-gone-wrong-5-fails-brands-can-learn-2-0888844.

17. "Facebook Gone Wrong," Business 2 Community.

CHAPTER 7: FACEBOOK

1. Ash Read, "The State of Social 2018 Report: Your Guide to Latest Social Media Marketing Research [New Data]," Buffer, updated January 18, 2019, https://blog.bufferapp.com/state-of-social-2018.

2. Max Chafkin, "How to Kill a Great Idea!" *Inc.*, June 1, 2007, https://www
.inc.com/magazine/20070601/features-how-to-kill-a-great-idea.html.

3. Gil Press, "Why Facebook Triumphed Over All Other Social Networks,"
Forbes, April 8, 2018, https://www.forbes.com/sites/gilpress/2018/04/08
/why-facebook-triumphed-over-all-other-social-networks/#261cd6d46e91.

4. Craig Smith, "250 Amazing Facebook Statistics, History and Facts (2019)
| By the Numbers," DMR, updated April 14, 2019, https://expandedramblings
.com/index.php/by-the-numbers-17-amazing-facebook-stats/.

5. Money Saving Mom (@moneysavingmom), Facebook, https://www
.facebook.com/MoneySavingMom.

6. Sophia Bernazzani, "The Decline of Organic Facebook Reach & How to
Adjust to the Algorithm," HubSpot, updated March 26, 2019, https://blog
.hubspot.com/marketing/facebook-organic-reach-declining.

7. Mark Zuckerberg (@zuck), "One of our big focus areas for 2018,"
Facebook, January 11, 2018, https://www.facebook.com/zuck/posts
/10104413015393571.

8. Bernazzani, "The Decline of Organic Facebook Reach."

9. Smith, "250 Amazing Facebook Statistics."

10. Brandon Leibowitz, "Instagram vs Facebook: Which Can Boost Your
Business More?," DreamGrow, July 9, 2018, https://www.dreamgrow.com
/instagram-facebook-advertising/.

11. Bernazzani, "The Decline of Organic Facebook Reach."

12. Alfred Lua, "Why I Think Social Media Is for Branding and Engagement,
Not Traffic or Revenue," Buffer, updated July 24, 2017, https://blog
.bufferapp.com/social-media-is-for-branding.

13. Alfred Lua, "7 Facebook Messenger Marketing Strategies You Can Try
Today," Buffer, updated December 3, 2018, https://blog.bufferapp.com
/facebook-messenger-marketing.

14. Lua, "7 Facebook Messenger Marketing Strategies."

15. Molly Pittman, "Facebook Messenger Ads: How to Use Them in Your
Business," Digital Marketer, September 6, 2018, https://www.digitalmarketer
.com/blog/how-to-use-facebook-messenger-ads/.

16. LEGO, "Increasing Sales Conversions with a Bot for Messenger," Facebook
Business, accessed April 15, 2019, https://www.facebook.com/business
/success/2-lego.

17. Smith, "250 Amazing Facebook Statistics."

18. Smith, "250 Amazing Facebook Statistics."

19. Read, "The State of Social 2018 Report."

20. Bernazzani, "The Decline of Organic Facebook Reach."

21. MyFo TriSport (@MyFo TriSport), Facebook, October 9, 2018, https://www.facebook.com/105352496713414/posts/10106556588221535.

22. MyFo TriSport (@MyFo TriSport), Facebook, October 17, 2018, https://www.facebook.com/105352496713414/posts/10106576754353445.

23. MyFo TriSport (@MyFo TriSport), "App," Facebook, October 17, 2018, https://www.facebook.com/105352496713414/posts/10106576754138875.

24. Amy Porterfield (@AmyPorterfield), Facebook, accessed March 7, 2019, https://www.facebook.com/AmyPorterfield/.

25. Amy Porterfield (@AmyPorterfield), Facebook, accessed March 28, 2019, https://www.facebook.com/AmyPorterfield/.

CHAPTER 8: INSTAGRAM

1. Kathleen Chaykowski, "Mark Zuckerberg Gains $1.7 Billion After Instagram Announces New 'TV' App, 1 Billion Users," *Forbes*, June 20, 2018, https://www.forbes.com/sites/kathleenchaykowski/2018/06/20/mark-zuckerberg-gains-1-7-billion-after-instagram-announces-new-tv-app-1-billion-users/#5dc9faa36a04.

2. Craig Smith, "250 Amazing Instagram Statistics and Facts (2019) | By the Numbers," DMR, updated Aril 15, 2019, https://expandedramblings.com/index.php/important-instagram-stats/.

3. Leibowitz, "Instagram vs Facebook" (see chap. 7, n. 10).

4. Away (@away), Instagram, September 10, 2018, https://www.instagram.com/p/BnkNWoVlSVp/.

5. Lisa-Jo Baker, "About," Lisa-Jo Baker (website), accessed April 30, 2019, http://lisajobaker.com/about-lisa-jo-baker/.

6. Baker, "About."

7. Jen Hatmaker (@jenhatmaker), "I didn't take any pics of our 25 member Thanksgiving feast today because I never have my phone out," Instagram, November 22, 2018, https://www.instagram.com/p/Bqgf6mzl0el/.

8. Lysa TerKeurst (@lysaterkeurst), Instagram, November 17, 2018, https://www.instagram.com/p/BqTPFiOlslA/.

9. Mailchimp (@mailchimp), "Grand hats for grandparents," Instagram, September 7, 2018, https://www.instagram.com/p/BnbSRnFnM4g/; Mailchimp, "[globe, trophy, monkey emoji]," Instagram, June 19, 2017, https://www.instagram.com/p/BViaRPbn3el/.

10. Pyne & Smith Clothiers (@pyneandsmithclothiers), Instagram, November 26, 2018, https://www.instagram.com/p/BqqrSW3l_6-/.

11. StoryBrand, (website), accessed April 30, 2019, https://storybrand.com/.

12. Cali'flour Foods (@califlourfoods), Instagram, November 10, 2018, https://www.instagram.com/p/BqBHHGyFSkk/; Cali'flour Foods, Instagram., November 10, 2018, https://www.instagram.com/p/BqBg_spFsl_/.

13. Ramit Sethi (@ramit), Instagram, January 2, 2019, https://www.instagram.com/p/BsI5vU1AqDP/.

14. South Shore Grill (@ssghawaii), Instagram, September 7, 2018, https://www.instagram.com/p/BncMaJgAj8r/.

15. Cotton Basics (@cottonbasics), Instagram, n.d., https://www.instagram.com/p/Burpsr3hx3A/ (post deleted).

16. Axe and the Oak Whiskey House (@axeandtheoak), Instagram, November 7, 2018, https://www.instagram.com/p/Bp5F7MQFsYm/; Axe and the Oak Whiskey House, Instagram, October 26, 2018, https://www.instagram.com/p/BpaelIHF4v1/.

17. Poncho Guitars (@ponchoguitars), "1955 #lespauljunior & 1958 #Esquire," Instagram, December 1, 2018, https://www.instagram.com/p/Bq3g1lenncK/; Poncho Guitars, "#teletuesday #tele #telecaster #customshop #guitar #guitars," Instagram, November 20, 2018, https://www.instagram.com/p/BqbF9Y-n2Vd/.

18. Jen Hatmaker (@jenhatmaker), Instagram, November 5, 2018, https://www.instagram.com/p/Bp0bZNUlabC/.

19. Joy Forney (@joyforney), Instagram, March 8, 2019, https://www.instagram.com/p/BuvuweABXAN/.

CHAPTER 9: TWITTER

1. Patagonia (@patagonia), "New report proves that three quarters of rivers in the Balkans are crucial life support systems for the entire ecosystem and should be totally off limits for hydropower," Twitter, November 28, 2018, 1:39 a.m., https://twitter.com/patagonia/status/1067714560856072192; Patagonia, "In a report released on #BlackFriday, take 10% off the size of the U.S. economy by 2100 from damage related to climate change," Twitter, November 28, 2018, 8:52 p.m., https://twitter.com/patagonia/status/1066192829943140354; Patagonia, "Love the outdoors? Here are 8 Senate races where we can make the difference," November 1, 2018, 1:49 p.m., https://twitter.com/patagonia/status/1058098794607337473.

2. Everlane (@everlane), Twitter, November 6, 2018, 10:46 a.m., https://twitter
   .com/Everlane/status/1059879779111862272.

3. World Vision (@WorldVision), Twitter, November 26, 2018, 2:44 a.m.,
   https://twitter.com/WorldVision/status/1067006238960087040.

4. Failed Missionary (@failmissionary), Twitter, November 27, 2018, 8:22 a.m.,
   https://twitter.com/failmissionary/status/1067453666771259398.

5. Missy, Master of the Slippery Slope (@aslipperyslope2), Twitter,
   November 27, 2018, 8:13 p.m., https://twitter.com/aslipperyslope2/status
   /1067632662154788864; Kevin Manuel García (@thekveingarcia_),
   Twitter, November 27, 2018, 9:34 a.m., https://twitter.com
   /theKevinGarcia_/status/1067471636318887937.

6. Ronald Baking (@RnBaking), Twitter, November 26, 2018, 11:22 p.m.,
   https://twitter.com/RnBaking/status/1067317612391075840.

7. Cali'flour Foods (@califlourfoods), Twitter, November 21, 2018, 7:09 a.m.,
   https://twitter.com/Califlourfoods/status/1065260910917210112.

CHAPTER 10: LINKEDIN

1. Craig Smith, "220 Amazing LinkedIn Statistics and Facts (2019) | By the
   Numbers," DMR, updated April 13, 2019, https://expandedramblings.com
   /index.php/by-the-numbers-a-few-important-linkedin-stats/.

2. Leibowitz, "Instagram vs Facebook" (see chap. 7, n. 10).

3. Oren Greenberg, "4 LinkedIn Mini Case Studies," Social Media Examiner,
   June 28, 2017, https://www.socialmediaexaminer.com/4-linkedin-mini
   -case-studies/.

4. David Kenny, "Why We Need Pioneers in Cognitive Computing," Venture
   Beat, January 24, 2017, https://venturebeat.com/2017/01/24/why-we
   -need-pioneers-in-cognitive-computing/.

5. Daniel Schreiber, "The Lemonade Transparency Chronicles," Lemonade,
   January 10, 2017, https://www.lemonade.com/blog/lemonade-transparency
   -chronicles/.

6. "Lemonade Case Study," LinkedIn Marketing Solutions, accessed April 15,
   2019, https://business.linkedin.com/marketing-solutions/case-studies
   /lemonade.

7. Jane Fleming, "What's the Best Time to Post on LinkedIn?," LinkedIn,
   July 13, 2016, https://business.linkedin.com/en-uk/marketing-solutions
   /blog/posts/B2B-Marketing/2016/Whats-the-best-time-to-post-on
   -LinkedIn.

8. Admin, "5 LinkedIn Case Studies That Got Results for Zero Spend," Our Social Times, accessed April 11, 2019, https://oursocialtimes.com /linkedin-marketing-5-businesses-that-got-big-results-with-zero-spend/.

9. "15 Tips for Compelling Company Updates," LinkedIn, accessed April 16, 2019, https://business.linkedin.com/content/dam/business/marketing -solutions/global/en_US/site/subsites/content-marketing/img/V2/e3 _Infographic_Draft_11_1200.pdf; "Lemonade Case Study," LinkedIn Marketing Solutions.

10. Greenberg, "4 LinkedIn Mini Case Studies."

11. Greenberg, "4 LinkedIn Mini Case Studies."

12. Smith, "220 Amazing LinkedIn Statistics."

13. Entrepreneurs HQ, "Celebrity Photographer Jeremy Cowart Analyzes His Own LinkedIn Photo at LinkedIn Success Summit," December 5, 2015, YouTube video, 1:33, https://www.youtube.com/watch?v=oIgm7RhecyY.

14. Smith, "220 Amazing LinkedIn Statistics."

15. Whitney Johnson, *Build an A-Team: Play to Their Strengths and Lead Them Up the Learning Curve* (Boston: Harvard Business School Publishing, 2018).

CHAPTER 11: COMPLEMENTARY PLATFORMS

1. Erica Chan Coffman (@HonestlyWTF), "Discover ideas about Nursery Room Ideas," Pinterest, March 2019, https://ar.pinterest.com/pin /54817320451335806/.

2. Ruth Soukup, "One Pot Pasta with Spinach & Sausage," Pinterest, accessed May 7, 2019, https://ar.pinterest.com/pin/567735096776397611/.

3. Ruth Soukup (@Elite Blog Academy), "4 Reasons Why Your Blog Is Failing," Pinterest, accessed May 7, 2019, https://ar.pinterest.com/pin /786370784915016044/.

4. Craig Smith, "12 Interesting Quora Statistics and Facts (2019) | By the Numbers," DMR, updated January 26, 2019, https://expandedramblings .com/index.php/quora-statistics/.

5. Elise Moreau, "What Exactly Is a Reddit AMA?," Lifewire, updated December 11, 2018, https://www.lifewire.com/what-exactly-is-a-reddit -ama-3485985.

6. chickensunited, "I'm coming to the end of 3 years teaching in the Brunei jungle, Borneo AMA," Reddit, December 2018, https://www.reddit .com/r/AMA/comments/a0jrt2/im_coming_to_the_end_of_3_years _teaching_in_the/; User deleted, "My rat's hands work on my phone screen,

I'm gonna let her answer some questions," Reddit, December 2018, https://www.reddit.com/r/AMA/comments/a0geg3/my_rats_hands _work_on_my_phone_screen_im_gonna/.

7. Brent Csutoras, "How to Host a Successful Reddit AMA," SEMrush, May 7, 2018, https://www.semrush.com/blog/how-to-host-a-successful-reddit -ama/.

8. Csutoras, "How to Host a Successful Reddit AMA."

9. Matt Weinberger, "Bill Gates' Wicked Sense of Humor Really Shines on Reddit—See for Yourself," *Business Insider*, February 27, 2017, https://www .businessinsider.com/bill-gates-reddit-ama-verification-photos-2017-2.

10. Bill Gates, "My Third AMA," Gates Notes, February 5, 2015, https://www .gatesnotes.com/About-Bill-Gates/2015-Reddit-AMA.

11. Taylor Soper, "Bill Gates Delivers Another Epic Secret Santa Gift to a Lucky Reddit User, with Help from Hank Green," GeekWire, December 22, 2018, https://www.geekwire.com/2018/bill-gates-delivers-another-epic-secret -santa-gift-lucky-reddit-user-help-hank-green/.

12. Paige Breaux, "What Hank and John Green's YouTube Community Can Teach Us About Video Marketing," Skyword, July 12, 2018, https://www .skyword.com/contentstandard/marketing/what-hank-and-john-greens -youtube-community-can-teach-us-about-video-marketing/.

13. Garrett Robinson, "8 Questions with Pro Internet Guy Hank Green of the Vlog Brothers," Sterling & Stone, accessed April 16, 2019, https://sterlingandstone.net/8-questions-hank-green-vlog-brothers/.

14. Breaux, "Hank and John Green's YouTube Community."

15. Breaux, "Hank and John Green's YouTube Community."

ABOUT THE AUTHOR

Claire Diaz-Ortiz is an innovation advisor, speaker, and start-up investor who was an early employee at Twitter. Named one of the 100 Most Creative People in Business by *Fast Company* and called "The Woman Who Got the Pope on Twitter" by *Wired*, she has written nine books that have been published in more than a dozen countries. Claire holds an MBA and other degrees from Stanford and Oxford and lives with her family in Buenos Aires.